Published Books
Tracker

for Self-Publishing Authors

eDiY
Biz Tools

eDiY Publishing

My Book Publishing Biz Profile

Tracker Period: from _____ to _____
Tracker Number: # _____

My Publisher Names	My Pen Names
• _____	• _____
• _____	• _____
• _____	• _____
• _____	• _____
• _____	• _____
• _____	• _____
• _____	• _____
• _____	• _____

Important Numbers

Tax Number   _____

Business Trading _____

_____   _____

_____   _____

Banking

Name	Type	Branch Code	Account Number
_____	_____	_____ - _____	_____
_____	_____	_____ - _____	_____
_____	_____	_____ - _____	_____
_____	_____	_____ - _____	_____

Other Important Numbers

_____

_____

My Book Publishing Biz Profile

My Direct Publishing Accounts

1. KDP (Amazon)   Email _____
                    p/w or hint _____

2. IngramSpark   Email _____
                    p/w or hint _____

3. _____ Email _____
                    p/w or hint _____

4. _____ Email _____
                    p/w or hint _____

5. _____ Email _____
                    p/w or hint _____

6. _____ Email _____
                    p/w or hint _____

7. _____ Email _____
                    p/w or hint _____

8. _____ Email _____
                    p/w or hint _____

9. _____ Email _____
                    p/w or hint _____

10. _____ Email _____
                    p/w or hint _____

Self-Published Books Tracker

Formats Available

Paperback	978-0-6486715-2-7
Hardcover	978-0-6486715-3-4

Image Credits

This publication may use, with our sincerest gratitude, commercial use permitted images sourced from **Pixabay** and **Freepik.**

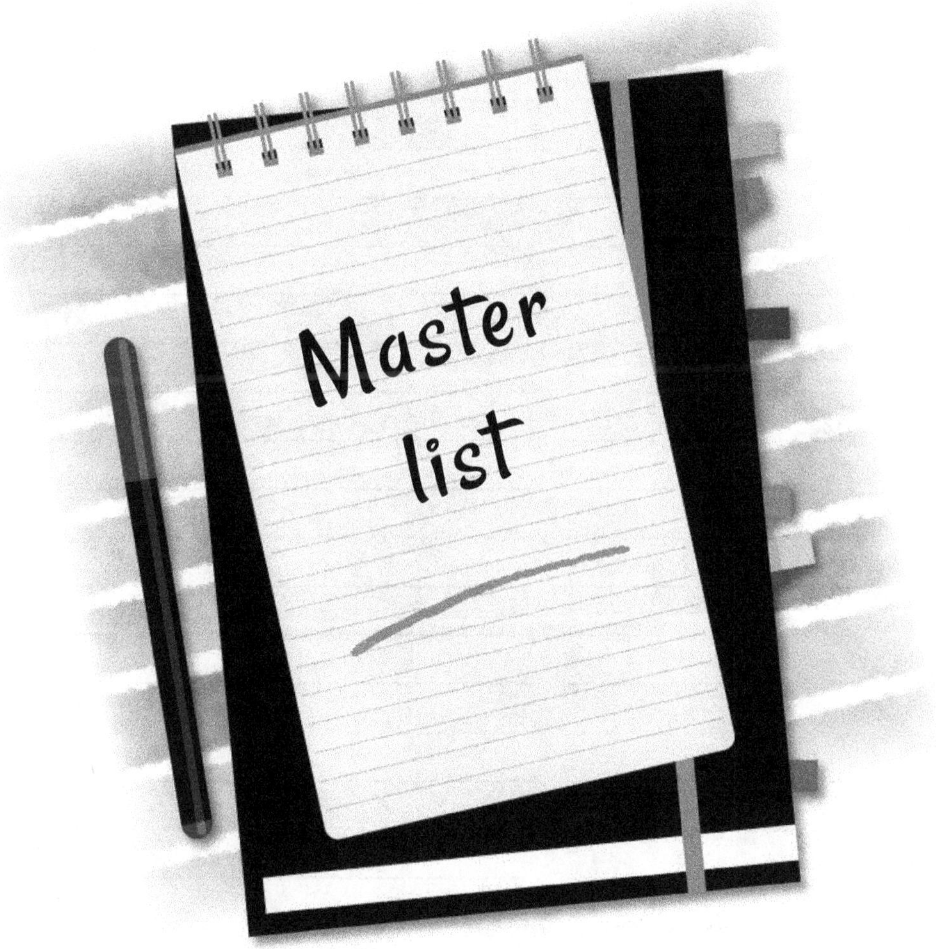
Master
list

Books Published Master List

	ISBN	Title
1		
2		
3		
4		
5		
6		
7		
8		
9		
10		
11		
12		
13		
14		
15		
16		
17		
18		
19		
20		
21		
22		
23		
24		
25		

Books Published Master List

Book Type	Date Published	Price	Royalty	Distribution Channel		Date Unpublished
_____	__/__/__	$_____	$_____	_____	☐	__/__/__
_____	__/__/__	$_____	$_____	_____	☐	__/__/__
_____	__/__/__	$_____	$_____	_____	☐	__/__/__
_____	__/__/__	$_____	$_____	_____	☐	__/__/__
_____	__/__/__	$_____	$_____	_____	☐	__/__/__
_____	__/__/__	$_____	$_____	_____	☐	__/__/__
_____	__/__/__	$_____	$_____	_____	☐	__/__/__
_____	__/__/__	$_____	$_____	_____	☐	__/__/__
_____	__/__/__	$_____	$_____	_____	☐	__/__/__
_____	__/__/__	$_____	$_____	_____	☐	__/__/__
_____	__/__/__	$_____	$_____	_____	☐	__/__/__
_____	__/__/__	$_____	$_____	_____	☐	__/__/__
_____	__/__/__	$_____	$_____	_____	☐	__/__/__
_____	__/__/__	$_____	$_____	_____	☐	__/__/__
_____	__/__/__	$_____	$_____	_____	☐	__/__/__
_____	__/__/__	$_____	$_____	_____	☐	__/__/__
_____	__/__/__	$_____	$_____	_____	☐	__/__/__
_____	__/__/__	$_____	$_____	_____	☐	__/__/__
_____	__/__/__	$_____	$_____	_____	☐	__/__/__
_____	__/__/__	$_____	$_____	_____	☐	__/__/__
_____	__/__/__	$_____	$_____	_____	☐	__/__/__
_____	__/__/__	$_____	$_____	_____	☐	__/__/__
_____	__/__/__	$_____	$_____	_____	☐	__/__/__
_____	__/__/__	$_____	$_____	_____	☐	__/__/__
_____	__/__/__	$_____	$_____	_____	☐	__/__/__

Books Published Master List

	ISBN	Title
26		
27		
28		
29		
30		
31		
32		
33		
34		
35		
36		
37		
38		
39		
40		
41		
42		
43		
44		
45		
46		
47		
48		
49		
50		

Books Published Master List

Book Type	Date Published	Price	Royalty	Distribution Channel		Date Unpublished
_____	__/__/__	$_____	$_____	_____	☐	__/__/__
_____	__/__/__	$_____	$_____	_____	☐	__/__/__
_____	__/__/__	$_____	$_____	_____	☐	__/__/__
_____	__/__/__	$_____	$_____	_____	☐	__/__/__
_____	__/__/__	$_____	$_____	_____	☐	__/__/__
_____	__/__/__	$_____	$_____	_____	☐	__/__/__
_____	__/__/__	$_____	$_____	_____	☐	__/__/__
_____	__/__/__	$_____	$_____	_____	☐	__/__/__
_____	__/__/__	$_____	$_____	_____	☐	__/__/__
_____	__/__/__	$_____	$_____	_____	☐	__/__/__
_____	__/__/__	$_____	$_____	_____	☐	__/__/__
_____	__/__/__	$_____	$_____	_____	☐	__/__/__
_____	__/__/__	$_____	$_____	_____	☐	__/__/__
_____	__/__/__	$_____	$_____	_____	☐	__/__/__
_____	__/__/__	$_____	$_____	_____	☐	__/__/__
_____	__/__/__	$_____	$_____	_____	☐	__/__/__
_____	__/__/__	$_____	$_____	_____	☐	__/__/__
_____	__/__/__	$_____	$_____	_____	☐	__/__/__
_____	__/__/__	$_____	$_____	_____	☐	__/__/__
_____	__/__/__	$_____	$_____	_____	☐	__/__/__
_____	__/__/__	$_____	$_____	_____	☐	__/__/__
_____	__/__/__	$_____	$_____	_____	☐	__/__/__
_____	__/__/__	$_____	$_____	_____	☐	__/__/__
_____	__/__/__	$_____	$_____	_____	☐	__/__/__
_____	__/__/__	$_____	$_____	_____	☐	__/__/__

Books Published Master List

	ISBN	Title
51		
52		
53		
54		
55		
56		
57		
58		
59		
60		
61		
62		
63		
64		
65		
66		
67		
68		
69		
70		
71		
72		
73		
74		
75		

Books Published Master List

Book Type	Date Published	Price	Royalty	Distribution Channel		Date Unpublished
_____	__/__/__	$_____	$_____	_____	☐	__/__/__
_____	__/__/__	$_____	$_____	_____	☐	__/__/__
_____	__/__/__	$_____	$_____	_____	☐	__/__/__
_____	__/__/__	$_____	$_____	_____	☐	__/__/__
_____	__/__/__	$_____	$_____	_____	☐	__/__/__
_____	__/__/__	$_____	$_____	_____	☐	__/__/__
_____	__/__/__	$_____	$_____	_____	☐	__/__/__
_____	__/__/__	$_____	$_____	_____	☐	__/__/__
_____	__/__/__	$_____	$_____	_____	☐	__/__/__
_____	__/__/__	$_____	$_____	_____	☐	__/__/__
_____	__/__/__	$_____	$_____	_____	☐	__/__/__
_____	__/__/__	$_____	$_____	_____	☐	__/__/__
_____	__/__/__	$_____	$_____	_____	☐	__/__/__
_____	__/__/__	$_____	$_____	_____	☐	__/__/__
_____	__/__/__	$_____	$_____	_____	☐	__/__/__
_____	__/__/__	$_____	$_____	_____	☐	__/__/__
_____	__/__/__	$_____	$_____	_____	☐	__/__/__
_____	__/__/__	$_____	$_____	_____	☐	__/__/__
_____	__/__/__	$_____	$_____	_____	☐	__/__/__
_____	__/__/__	$_____	$_____	_____	☐	__/__/__
_____	__/__/__	$_____	$_____	_____	☐	__/__/__
_____	__/__/__	$_____	$_____	_____	☐	__/__/__
_____	__/__/__	$_____	$_____	_____	☐	__/__/__
_____	__/__/__	$_____	$_____	_____	☐	__/__/__
_____	__/__/__	$_____	$_____	_____	☐	__/__/__

Books Published Master List

	ISBN	Title
76		
77		
78		
79		
80		
81		
82		
83		
84		
85		
86		
87		
88		
89		
90		
91		
92		
93		
94		
95		
96		
97		
98		
99		
100		

Books Published Master List

Book Type	Date Published	Price	Royalty	Distribution Channel		Date Unpublished
_____	__/__/__	$_____	$_____	_____	☐	__/__/__
_____	__/__/__	$_____	$_____	_____	☐	__/__/__
_____	__/__/__	$_____	$_____	_____	☐	__/__/__
_____	__/__/__	$_____	$_____	_____	☐	__/__/__
_____	__/__/__	$_____	$_____	_____	☐	__/__/__
_____	__/__/__	$_____	$_____	_____	☐	__/__/__
_____	__/__/__	$_____	$_____	_____	☐	__/__/__
_____	__/__/__	$_____	$_____	_____	☐	__/__/__
_____	__/__/__	$_____	$_____	_____	☐	__/__/__
_____	__/__/__	$_____	$_____	_____	☐	__/__/__
_____	__/__/__	$_____	$_____	_____	☐	__/__/__
_____	__/__/__	$_____	$_____	_____	☐	__/__/__
_____	__/__/__	$_____	$_____	_____	☐	__/__/__
_____	__/__/__	$_____	$_____	_____	☐	__/__/__
_____	__/__/__	$_____	$_____	_____	☐	__/__/__
_____	__/__/__	$_____	$_____	_____	☐	__/__/__
_____	__/__/__	$_____	$_____	_____	☐	__/__/__
_____	__/__/__	$_____	$_____	_____	☐	__/__/__
_____	__/__/__	$_____	$_____	_____	☐	__/__/__
_____	__/__/__	$_____	$_____	_____	☐	__/__/__
_____	__/__/__	$_____	$_____	_____	☐	__/__/__
_____	__/__/__	$_____	$_____	_____	☐	__/__/__
_____	__/__/__	$_____	$_____	_____	☐	__/__/__
_____	__/__/__	$_____	$_____	_____	☐	__/__/__
_____	__/__/__	$_____	$_____	_____	☐	__/__/__

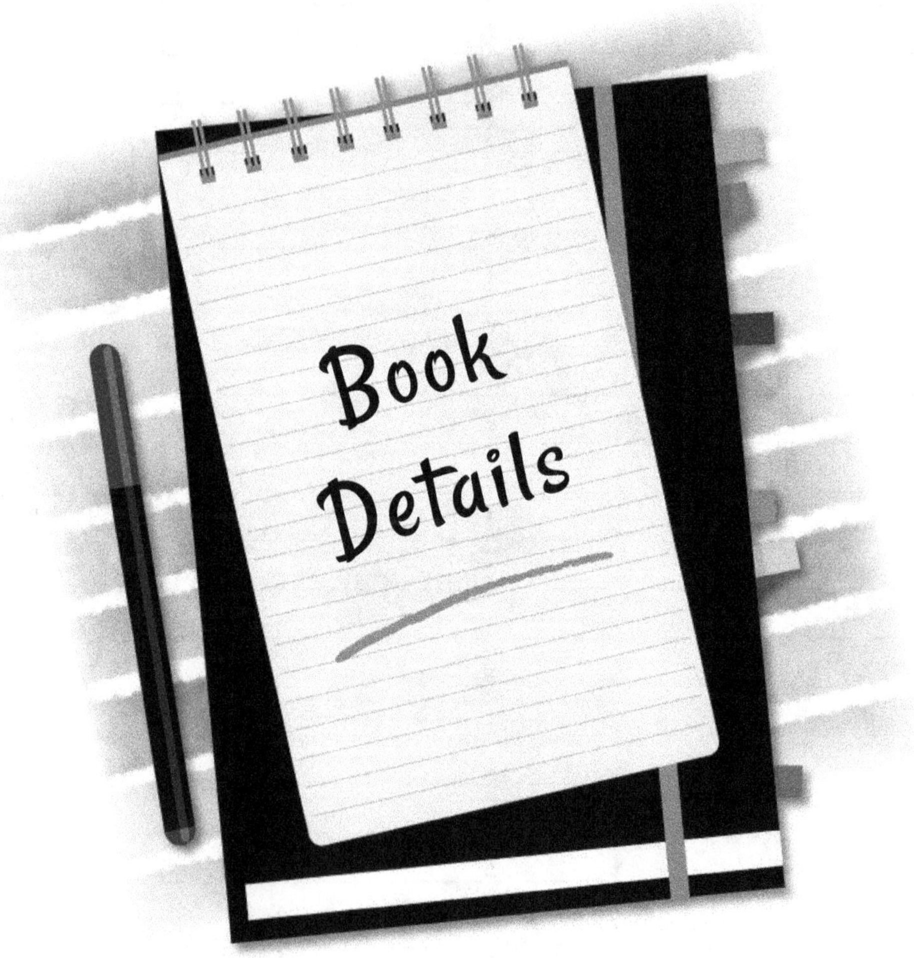
Book
Details

Title Details

Title _____

Subtitle _____

ISBN _____ - _____

Book Type ☐ eBook ☐ Paperback
☐ Hardcover ☐ Audiobook
☐ Shareable PDF

Version _____ Edition _____

Series _____

Page Count _____ Trim Size _____ x _____

Date Published ____/____/____ = Q1 Q2 Q3 Q4

Publisher ☐ KDP ☐ KDP Print ☐ IngramSpark

Account(s) ☐ _____ ☐ _____
☐ _____ ☐ _____

Price $_____ Currency _____

Markets ☐ Global ☐ _____ ☐ _____
☐ _____ ☐ _____ ☐ _____

Categories 1. _____
2. _____

Keywords 1. _____
2. _____
3. _____
4. _____
5. _____
6. _____
7. _____

Book _____

Description _____

_____

Book Cover _____

Date First Sale ____/____/____ = Q1 Q2 Q3 Q4

☐ Unpublished on ____/____/____

2   **Title Details**

Title   _____

Subtitle   _____

ISBN   _____ - _____

Book Type   ☐ eBook   ☐ Paperback

              ☐ Hardcover   ☐ Audiobook

              ☐ Shareable PDF

Version   _____ Edition   _____

Series   _____

Page Count   _____ Trim Size   _____ x _____

Date Published   ____/____/____   =   Q1   Q2   Q3   Q4

Publisher   ☐ KDP   ☐ KDP Print   ☐ IngramSpark

Account(s)   ☐ _____   ☐ _____

            ☐ _____   ☐ _____

Price $_____   Currency _____

Markets   ☐ Global   ☐ _____   ☐ _____

          ☐ _____   ☐ _____   ☐ _____

Categories   1. _____

            2. _____

Keywords   1. _____

            2. _____

            3. _____

            4. _____

            5. _____

            6. _____

            7. _____

Book   _____

Description   _____

            _____

Book Cover   _____

Date First Sale   ____/____/____   =   Q1   Q2   Q3   Q4

                  ☐ Unpublished on ____/____/____

Title Details **3**

Title   _____

Subtitle   _____

ISBN   _____ - _____

Book Type
- ☐ eBook   ☐ Paperback
- ☐ Hardcover   ☐ Audiobook
- ☐ Shareable PDF

Version   _____   Edition   _____

Series   _____

Page Count   _____   Trim Size   _____ x _____

Date Published   ____/____/____   =   Q1   Q2   Q3   Q4

Publisher   ☐ KDP   ☐ KDP Print   ☐ IngramSpark

Account(s)
- ☐ _____   ☐ _____
- ☐ _____   ☐ _____

Price $_____   Currency _____

Markets
- ☐ Global   ☐ _____   ☐ _____
- ☐ _____   ☐ _____   ☐ _____

Categories
1. _____
2. _____

Keywords
1. _____
2. _____
3. _____
4. _____
5. _____
6. _____
7. _____

Book Description   _____
_____
_____

Book Cover   _____

Date First Sale   ____/____/____   =   Q1   Q2   Q3   Q4

     ☐ Unpublished on ____/____/____

4   **Title Details**

Title   _____

Subtitle   _____

ISBN   _____ - _____

Book Type   ☐ eBook   ☐ Paperback

              ☐ Hardcover   ☐ Audiobook

              ☐ Shareable PDF

Version   _____ Edition   _____

Series   _____

Page Count   _____ Trim Size   _____ x _____

Date Published   _____/_____/_____   =   Q1   Q2   Q3   Q4

Publisher   ☐ KDP   ☐ KDP Print   ☐ IngramSpark

Account(s)   ☐ _____   ☐ _____

            ☐ _____   ☐ _____

Price $_____ Currency _____

Markets   ☐ Global   ☐ _____   ☐ _____

         ☐ _____   ☐ _____   ☐ _____

Categories   1. _____

            2. _____

Keywords   1. _____

           2. _____

           3. _____

           4. _____

           5. _____

           6. _____

           7. _____

Book   _____

Description   _____

            _____

Book Cover   _____

Date First Sale   _____/_____/_____   =   Q1   Q2   Q3   Q4

                               ☐ Unpublished on _____/_____/_____

Title Details   **5**

Title   _____

Subtitle   _____

ISBN   _____ - _____

Book Type   ☐ eBook   ☐ Paperback
               ☐ Hardcover   ☐ Audiobook
               ☐ Shareable PDF

Version   _____ Edition _____

Series   _____

Page Count   _____ Trim Size _____ x _____

Date Published ___/___/___ = Q1   Q2   Q3   Q4

Publisher   ☐ KDP ☐ KDP Print   ☐ IngramSpark

Account(s)   ☐ _____   ☐ _____
               ☐ _____   ☐ _____

Price $_____ Currency _____

Markets   ☐ Global   ☐ _____ ☐ _____
               ☐ _____ ☐ _____ ☐ _____

Categories   1. _____
               2. _____

Keywords   1. _____
               2. _____
               3. _____
               4. _____
               5. _____
               6. _____
               7. _____

Book   _____
Description   _____
              _____

Book Cover   _____

Date First Sale ___/___/___ = Q1   Q2   Q3   Q4
                         ☐ Unpublished on ___/___/___

6   **Title Details**

Title _____

Subtitle _____

ISBN _____ - _____

Book Type
    ☐ eBook   ☐ Paperback
    ☐ Hardcover   ☐ Audiobook
    ☐ Shareable PDF

Version _____ Edition _____

Series _____

Page Count _____ Trim Size _____ x _____

Date Published ____/____/____ =   Q1   Q2   Q3   Q4

Publisher   ☐ KDP   ☐ KDP Print   ☐ IngramSpark

Account(s)
    ☐ _____   ☐ _____
    ☐ _____   ☐ _____

Price $_____ Currency _____

Markets
    ☐ Global   ☐ _____   ☐ _____
    ☐ _____   ☐ _____   ☐ _____

Categories
  1. _____
  2. _____

Keywords
  1. _____
  2. _____
  3. _____
  4. _____
  5. _____
  6. _____
  7. _____

Book
Description
_____
_____
_____

Book Cover _____

Date First Sale ____/____/____ =   Q1   Q2   Q3   Q4
                         ☐ Unpublished on ____/____/____

Title Details

Title _____

Subtitle _____

ISBN _____ - _____

Book Type   □ eBook   □ Paperback
             □ Hardcover   □ Audiobook
             □ Shareable PDF

Version   _____   Edition   _____

Series _____

Page Count   _____   Trim Size   _____ x _____

Date Published   ____/____/____   =   Q1   Q2   Q3   Q4

Publisher   □ KDP   □ KDP Print   □ IngramSpark

Account(s)   □ _____   □ _____
           □ _____   □ _____

Price $_____   Currency _____

Markets   □ Global   □ _____   □ _____
        □ _____   □ _____   □ _____

Categories   1. _____
           2. _____

Keywords   1. _____
           2. _____
           3. _____
           4. _____
           5. _____
           6. _____
           7. _____

Book _____

Description _____

_____

Book Cover _____

Date First Sale   ____/____/____   =   Q1   Q2   Q3   Q4
                 □ Unpublished on ____/____/____

8   **Title Details**

Title	_____
Subtitle	_____
ISBN	_____ - _____

Book Type   ☐ eBook   ☐ Paperback
                   ☐ Hardcover   ☐ Audiobook
                   ☐ Shareable PDF

Version   _____ Edition _____

Series   _____

Page Count   _____ Trim Size   _____ x _____

Date Published   ____/____/____ =   Q1   Q2   Q3   Q4

Publisher   ☐ KDP   ☐ KDP Print   ☐ IngramSpark

Account(s)   ☐ _____   ☐ _____
            ☐ _____   ☐ _____

Price $_____ Currency _____

Markets   ☐ Global   ☐ _____   ☐ _____
         ☐ _____   ☐ _____   ☐ _____

Categories   1. _____
           2. _____

Keywords   1. _____
          2. _____
          3. _____
          4. _____
          5. _____
          6. _____
          7. _____

Book   _____
Description   _____
            _____

Book Cover   _____

Date First Sale   ____/____/____   =   Q1   Q2   Q3   Q4
                ☐ Unpublished on ____/____/____

Title Details

Title _____

Subtitle _____

ISBN _____ - _____

Book Type
☐ eBook   ☐ Paperback
☐ Hardcover ☐ Audiobook
☐ Shareable PDF

Version _____ Edition _____

Series _____

Page Count _____ Trim Size _____ x _____

Date Published ____/____/____ = Q1 Q2 Q3 Q4

Publisher ☐ KDP ☐ KDP Print ☐ IngramSpark

Account(s)
☐ _____   ☐ _____
☐ _____   ☐ _____

Price $_____ Currency _____

Markets
☐ Global   ☐ _____ ☐ _____
☐ _____ ☐ _____ ☐ _____

Categories
1. _____
2. _____

Keywords
1. _____
2. _____
3. _____
4. _____
5. _____
6. _____
7. _____

Book Description _____
_____
_____

Book Cover _____

Date First Sale ____/____/____ = Q1 Q2 Q3 Q4
☐ Unpublished on ____/____/____

10

Title Details

Title _____

Subtitle _____

ISBN _____ - _____

Book Type   ☐ eBook   ☐ Paperback

             ☐ Hardcover   ☐ Audiobook

             ☐ Shareable PDF

Version _____ Edition _____

Series _____

Page Count _____ Trim Size _____ x _____

Date Published ____/____/____   =   Q1   Q2   Q3   Q4

Publisher   ☐ KDP   ☐ KDP Print   ☐ IngramSpark

Account(s)   ☐ _____   ☐ _____

            ☐ _____   ☐ _____

Price $_____   Currency _____

Markets   ☐ Global   ☐ _____   ☐ _____

         ☐ _____   ☐ _____   ☐ _____

Categories   1. _____

           2. _____

Keywords   1. _____

           2. _____

           3. _____

           4. _____

           5. _____

           6. _____

           7. _____

Book _____

Description _____

_____

Book Cover _____

Date First Sale ____/____/____   =   Q1   Q2   Q3   Q4

                         ☐ Unpublished on ____/____/____

Title Details 11

Title _____

Subtitle _____

ISBN _____ - _____

Book Type   ☐ eBook   ☐ Paperback
             ☐ Hardcover   ☐ Audiobook
             ☐ Shareable PDF

Version _____   Edition _____

Series _____

Page Count _____ Trim Size _____ x _____

Date Published ____/____/____   =   Q1   Q2   Q3   Q4

Publisher   ☐ KDP   ☐ KDP Print   ☐ IngramSpark

Account(s)   ☐ _____   ☐ _____
          ☐ _____   ☐ _____

Price $_____   Currency _____

Markets   ☐ Global   ☐ _____   ☐ _____
        ☐ _____   ☐ _____   ☐ _____

Categories   1. _____
             2. _____

Keywords   1. _____
            2. _____
            3. _____
            4. _____
            5. _____
            6. _____
            7. _____

Book _____

Description _____

_____

Book Cover _____

Date First Sale ____/____/____   =   Q1   Q2   Q3   Q4

                        ☐ Unpublished on ____/____/____

12   **Title Details**

Title   _____

Subtitle   _____

ISBN   _____ - _____

Book Type   ☐ eBook   ☐ Paperback

                     ☐ Hardcover   ☐ Audiobook

                     ☐ Shareable PDF

Version   _____ Edition   _____

Series   _____

Page Count   _____ Trim Size   _____ x _____

Date Published   ____/____/____   =   Q1   Q2   Q3   Q4

Publisher   ☐ KDP   ☐ KDP Print   ☐ IngramSpark

Account(s)   ☐ _____   ☐ _____

                     ☐ _____   ☐ _____

Price $_____   Currency _____

Markets   ☐ Global   ☐ _____   ☐ _____

                     ☐ _____   ☐ _____   ☐ _____

Categories   1. _____

                     2. _____

Keywords   1. _____

                     2. _____

                     3. _____

                     4. _____

                     5. _____

                     6. _____

                     7. _____

Book   _____

Description   _____

                     _____

Book Cover   _____

Date First Sale   ____/____/____   =   Q1   Q2   Q3   Q4

                                     ☐ Unpublished on ____/____/____

Title Details **13**

Title _____

Subtitle _____

ISBN _____ - _____

Book Type   □ eBook   □ Paperback
              □ Hardcover   □ Audiobook
              □ Shareable PDF

Version   _____   Edition   _____

Series _____

Page Count   _____   Trim Size   _____ x _____

Date Published   ____/____/____   =   Q1   Q2   Q3   Q4

Publisher   □ KDP   □ KDP Print   □ IngramSpark

Account(s)   □ _____   □ _____
            □ _____   □ _____

Price $_____   Currency _____

Markets   □ Global   □ _____   □ _____
        □ _____   □ _____   □ _____

Categories   1. _____
            2. _____

Keywords   1. _____
          2. _____
          3. _____
          4. _____
          5. _____
          6. _____
          7. _____

Book _____
Description _____
            _____

Book Cover _____

Date First Sale   ____/____/____   =   Q1   Q2   Q3   Q4
                        □ Unpublished on ____/____/____

14   **Title Details**

Title   _____

Subtitle   _____

ISBN   _____ - _____

Book Type   ☐ eBook   ☐ Paperback

               ☐ Hardcover   ☐ Audiobook

               ☐ Shareable PDF

Version   _____ Edition _____

Series   _____

Page Count   _____ Trim Size _____ x _____

Date Published   ____/____/____ =   Q1   Q2   Q3   Q4

Publisher   ☐ KDP   ☐ KDP Print   ☐ IngramSpark

Account(s)   ☐ _____   ☐ _____

              ☐ _____   ☐ _____

Price $_____ Currency _____

Markets   ☐ Global   ☐ _____   ☐ _____

            ☐ _____   ☐ _____   ☐ _____

Categories   1. _____

            2. _____

Keywords   1. _____

            2. _____

            3. _____

            4. _____

            5. _____

            6. _____

            7. _____

Book   _____

Description   _____

             _____

Book Cover   _____

Date First Sale   ____/____/____   =   Q1   Q2   Q3   Q4

                               ☐ Unpublished on ____/____/____

Title Details

Title _____

Subtitle _____

ISBN _____ - _____

Book Type
☐ eBook   ☐ Paperback
☐ Hardcover   ☐ Audiobook
☐ Shareable PDF

Version _____ Edition _____

Series _____

Page Count _____ Trim Size _____ x _____

Date Published ____/____/____ = | Q1 | Q2 | Q3 | Q4 |

Publisher ☐ KDP ☐ KDP Print ☐ IngramSpark

Account(s)
☐ _____   ☐ _____
☐ _____   ☐ _____

Price $_____ Currency _____

Markets
☐ Global   ☐ _____ ☐ _____
☐ _____ ☐ _____ ☐ _____

Categories
1. _____
2. _____

Keywords
1. _____
2. _____
3. _____
4. _____
5. _____
6. _____
7. _____

Book
Description
_____
_____
_____

Book Cover _____

Date First Sale ____/____/____ = | Q1 | Q2 | Q3 | Q4 |

☐ Unpublished on ____/____/____

16   **Title Details**

Title   _____

Subtitle   _____

ISBN   _____ - _____

Book Type   ☐ eBook   ☐ Paperback
                       ☐ Hardcover   ☐ Audiobook
                       ☐ Shareable PDF

Version   _____ Edition _____

Series   _____

Page Count   _____ Trim Size   _____ x _____

Date Published   ____/____/____ =   Q1   Q2   Q3   Q4

Publisher   ☐ KDP   ☐ KDP Print   ☐ IngramSpark

Account(s)   ☐ _____   ☐ _____
                      ☐ _____   ☐ _____

Price $_____ Currency _____

Markets   ☐ Global   ☐ _____   ☐ _____
                     ☐ _____   ☐ _____   ☐ _____

Categories   1. _____
                     2. _____

Keywords   1. _____
                     2. _____
                     3. _____
                     4. _____
                     5. _____
                     6. _____
                     7. _____

Book   _____

Description   _____
                     _____

Book Cover   _____

Date First Sale   ____/____/____   =   Q1   Q2   Q3   Q4
                                    ☐ Unpublished on ____/____/____

Title Details **17**

Title   _____

Subtitle   _____

ISBN   _____ - _____

Book Type   ☐ eBook   ☐ Paperback
                 ☐ Hardcover   ☐ Audiobook
                 ☐ Shareable PDF

Version   _____   Edition   _____

Series   _____

Page Count   _____   Trim Size   _____ x _____

Date Published   ____/____/____   =   Q1   Q2   Q3   Q4

Publisher   ☐ KDP   ☐ KDP Print   ☐ IngramSpark

Account(s)   ☐ _____   ☐ _____
             ☐ _____   ☐ _____

Price $_____   Currency _____

Markets   ☐ Global   ☐ _____   ☐ _____
         ☐ _____   ☐ _____   ☐ _____

Categories   1. _____
             2. _____

Keywords   1. _____
            2. _____
            3. _____
            4. _____
            5. _____
            6. _____
            7. _____

Book   _____

Description   _____
             _____

Book Cover   _____

Date First Sale   ____/____/____   =   Q1   Q2   Q3   Q4
                  ☐ Unpublished on ____/____/____

18   **Title Details**

Title   _____

Subtitle   _____

ISBN   _____ - _____

Book Type
- ☐ eBook   ☐ Paperback
- ☐ Hardcover   ☐ Audiobook
- ☐ Shareable PDF

Version   _____ Edition _____

Series   _____

Page Count   _____ Trim Size   _____ x _____

Date Published   _____/_____/_____   =   Q1   Q2   Q3   Q4

Publisher   ☐ KDP   ☐ KDP Print   ☐ IngramSpark

Account(s)
- ☐ _____   ☐ _____
- ☐ _____   ☐ _____

Price $_____ Currency _____

Markets
- ☐ Global   ☐ _____   ☐ _____
- ☐ _____   ☐ _____   ☐ _____

Categories
1. _____
2. _____

Keywords
1. _____
2. _____
3. _____
4. _____
5. _____
6. _____
7. _____

Book Description   _____

_____

_____

Book Cover   _____

Date First Sale   _____/_____/_____   =   Q1   Q2   Q3   Q4

☐ Unpublished on _____/_____/_____

Title Details   **19**

Title   _____

Subtitle   _____

ISBN   _____ - _____

Book Type   ☐ eBook   ☐ Paperback
             ☐ Hardcover   ☐ Audiobook
             ☐ Shareable PDF

Version   _____ Edition   _____

Series   _____

Page Count   _____ Trim Size   _____ x _____

Date Published   ___/___/___ =   Q1   Q2   Q3   Q4

Publisher   ☐ KDP ☐ KDP Print   ☐ IngramSpark

Account(s)   ☐ _____   ☐ _____
           ☐ _____   ☐ _____

Price $_____ Currency _____

Markets   ☐ Global   ☐ _____   ☐ _____
         ☐ _____   ☐ _____   ☐ _____

Categories   1. _____
           2. _____

Keywords   1. _____
           2. _____
           3. _____
           4. _____
           5. _____
           6. _____
           7. _____

Book
Description   _____
           _____
           _____

Book Cover   _____

Date First Sale   ___/___/___ =   Q1   Q2   Q3   Q4
           ☐ Unpublished on ___/___/___

20   **Title Details**

Title   _____

Subtitle   _____

ISBN   _____ - _____

Book Type   ☐ eBook   ☐ Paperback
                 ☐ Hardcover   ☐ Audiobook
                 ☐ Shareable PDF

Version   _____   Edition   _____

Series   _____

Page Count   _____   Trim Size   _____ x _____

Date Published   ____/____/____   =   Q1   Q2   Q3   Q4

Publisher   ☐ KDP   ☐ KDP Print   ☐ IngramSpark

Account(s)   ☐ _____   ☐ _____
              ☐ _____   ☐ _____

Price $_____   Currency _____

Markets   ☐ Global   ☐ _____   ☐ _____
              ☐ _____   ☐ _____   ☐ _____

Categories   1. _____
              2. _____

Keywords   1. _____
              2. _____
              3. _____
              4. _____
              5. _____
              6. _____
              7. _____

Book   _____

Description   _____

                 _____

Book Cover   _____

Date First Sale   ____/____/____   =   Q1   Q2   Q3   Q4
                      ☐ Unpublished on ____/____/____

Title Details

Title _____

Subtitle _____

ISBN _____ - _____

Book Type
☐ eBook ☐ Paperback
☐ Hardcover ☐ Audiobook
☐ Shareable PDF

Version _____ Edition _____

Series _____

Page Count _____ Trim Size _____ x _____

Date Published ____/____/____ = Q1 Q2 Q3 Q4

Publisher ☐ KDP ☐ KDP Print ☐ IngramSpark

Account(s)
☐ _____ ☐ _____
☐ _____ ☐ _____

Price $_____ Currency _____

Markets
☐ Global ☐ _____ ☐ _____
☐ _____ ☐ _____ ☐ _____

Categories
1. _____
2. _____

Keywords
1. _____
2. _____
3. _____
4. _____
5. _____
6. _____
7. _____

Book
Description
_____
_____
_____

Book Cover _____

Date First Sale ____/____/____ = Q1 Q2 Q3 Q4
☐ Unpublished on ____/____/____

22   **Title Details**

Title   _____

Subtitle   _____

ISBN   _____ - _____

Book Type   ☐ eBook   ☐ Paperback

                        ☐ Hardcover   ☐ Audiobook

                        ☐ Shareable PDF

Version   _____   Edition   _____

Series   _____

Page Count   _____   Trim Size   _____ x _____

Date Published   ____/____/____   =   Q1   Q2   Q3   Q4

Publisher   ☐ KDP   ☐ KDP Print   ☐ IngramSpark

Account(s)   ☐ _____   ☐ _____

                    ☐ _____   ☐ _____

Price $_____   Currency _____

Markets   ☐ Global   ☐ _____   ☐ _____

                    ☐ _____   ☐ _____   ☐ _____

Categories   1. _____

                    2. _____

Keywords   1. _____

                    2. _____

                    3. _____

                    4. _____

                    5. _____

                    6. _____

                    7. _____

Book   _____

Description   _____

                    _____

Book Cover   _____

Date First Sale   ____/____/____   =   Q1   Q2   Q3   Q4

                                  ☐ Unpublished on ____/____/____

Title Details   **23**

Title   _____

Subtitle   _____

ISBN   _____ - _____

Book Type
- ☐ eBook   ☐ Paperback
- ☐ Hardcover   ☐ Audiobook
- ☐ Shareable PDF

Version   _____ Edition   _____

Series   _____

Page Count   _____ Trim Size   _____ x _____

Date Published   ____/____/____ = Q1   Q2   Q3   Q4

Publisher   ☐ KDP   ☐ KDP Print   ☐ IngramSpark

Account(s)
- ☐ _____   ☐ _____
- ☐ _____   ☐ _____

Price $_____ Currency _____

Markets
- ☐ Global   ☐ _____   ☐ _____
- ☐ _____   ☐ _____   ☐ _____

Categories
1. _____
2. _____

Keywords
1. _____
2. _____
3. _____
4. _____
5. _____
6. _____
7. _____

Book Description   _____
_____
_____
_____

Book Cover   _____

Date First Sale   ____/____/____ = Q1   Q2   Q3   Q4

☐ Unpublished on ____/____/____

24   **Title Details**

Title _____

Subtitle _____

ISBN _____ - _____

Book Type
- ☐ eBook ☐ Paperback
- ☐ Hardcover ☐ Audiobook
- ☐ Shareable PDF

Version _____ Edition _____

Series _____

Page Count _____ Trim Size _____ x _____

Date Published ___/___/___ = Q1 Q2 Q3 Q4

Publisher ☐ KDP ☐ KDP Print ☐ IngramSpark

Account(s)
- ☐ _____ ☐ _____
- ☐ _____ ☐ _____

Price $_____ Currency _____

Markets
- ☐ Global ☐ _____ ☐ _____
- ☐ _____ ☐ _____ ☐ _____

Categories
1. _____
2. _____

Keywords
1. _____
2. _____
3. _____
4. _____
5. _____
6. _____
7. _____

Book Description _____
_____
_____

Book Cover _____

Date First Sale ___/___/___ = Q1 Q2 Q3 Q4

☐ Unpublished on ___/___/___

Title Details

Title _____

Subtitle _____

ISBN _____ - _____

Book Type   ☐ eBook   ☐ Paperback
            ☐ Hardcover   ☐ Audiobook
            ☐ Shareable PDF

Version _____ Edition _____

Series _____

Page Count _____ Trim Size _____ x _____

Date Published ____/____/____ =   Q1   Q2   Q3   Q4

Publisher   ☐ KDP   ☐ KDP Print   ☐ IngramSpark

Account(s)   ☐ _____   ☐ _____
            ☐ _____   ☐ _____

Price $_____ Currency _____

Markets   ☐ Global   ☐ _____   ☐ _____
          ☐ _____   ☐ _____   ☐ _____

Categories   1. _____
           2. _____

Keywords   1. _____
          2. _____
          3. _____
          4. _____
          5. _____
          6. _____
          7. _____

Book _____

Description _____

_____

Book Cover _____

Date First Sale   ____/____/____   =   Q1   Q2   Q3   Q4
                      ☐ Unpublished on ____/____/____

26 **Title Details**

Title _____

Subtitle _____

ISBN _____ - _____

Book Type ☐ eBook   ☐ Paperback
☐ Hardcover   ☐ Audiobook
☐ Shareable PDF

Version _____ Edition _____

Series _____

Page Count _____ Trim Size _____ x _____

Date Published ____/____/____ = Q1   Q2   Q3   Q4

Publisher ☐ KDP ☐ KDP Print   ☐ IngramSpark

Account(s) ☐ _____   ☐ _____
☐ _____   ☐ _____

Price $_____ Currency _____

Markets ☐ Global   ☐ _____   ☐ _____
☐ _____   ☐ _____   ☐ _____

Categories 1. _____
2. _____

Keywords 1. _____
2. _____
3. _____
4. _____
5. _____
6. _____
7. _____

Book
Description _____
_____
_____

Book Cover _____

Date First Sale ____/____/____ = Q1   Q2   Q3   Q4
☐ Unpublished on ____/____/____

Title Details

Title	_____
Subtitle	_____
ISBN	_____ - _____

Book Type
- ☐ eBook   ☐ Paperback
- ☐ Hardcover   ☐ Audiobook
- ☐ Shareable PDF

Version _____ Edition _____

Series _____

Page Count _____ Trim Size _____ x _____

Date Published ____/____/____ = Q1   Q2   Q3   Q4

Publisher ☐ KDP ☐ KDP Print   ☐ IngramSpark

Account(s)
- ☐ _____   ☐ _____
- ☐ _____   ☐ _____

Price $_____ Currency _____

Markets
- ☐ Global   ☐ _____   ☐ _____
- ☐ _____   ☐ _____   ☐ _____

Categories
1. _____
2. _____

Keywords
1. _____
2. _____
3. _____
4. _____
5. _____
6. _____
7. _____

Book
Description
_____
_____
_____

Book Cover _____

Date First Sale ____/____/____ = Q1   Q2   Q3   Q4

☐ Unpublished on ____/____/____

28   **Title Details**

Title   _____

Subtitle   _____

ISBN   _____ - _____

Book Type
     ☐ eBook   ☐ Paperback
     ☐ Hardcover   ☐ Audiobook
     ☐ Shareable PDF

Version   _____ Edition   _____

Series   _____

Page Count   _____ Trim Size   _____ x _____

Date Published   ____/____/____   =   Q1   Q2   Q3   Q4

Publisher   ☐ KDP   ☐ KDP Print   ☐ IngramSpark

Account(s)
     ☐ _____   ☐ _____
     ☐ _____   ☐ _____

Price $_____ Currency _____

Markets
     ☐ Global   ☐ _____   ☐ _____
     ☐ _____   ☐ _____   ☐ _____

Categories
    1. _____
    2. _____

Keywords
    1. _____
    2. _____
    3. _____
    4. _____
    5. _____
    6. _____
    7. _____

Book
Description
    _____
    _____
    _____

Book Cover   _____

Date First Sale   ____/____/____   =   Q1   Q2   Q3   Q4

               ☐ Unpublished on ____/____/____

Title Details

Title _____

Subtitle _____

ISBN _____ - _____

Book Type   ☐ eBook   ☐ Paperback
              ☐ Hardcover   ☐ Audiobook
              ☐ Shareable PDF

Version _____ Edition _____

Series _____

Page Count _____ Trim Size _____ x _____

Date Published ___/___/___ =   Q1   Q2   Q3   Q4

Publisher   ☐ KDP   ☐ KDP Print   ☐ IngramSpark

Account(s)   ☐ _____   ☐ _____
           ☐ _____   ☐ _____

Price $_____ Currency _____

Markets   ☐ Global   ☐ _____   ☐ _____
        ☐ _____   ☐ _____   ☐ _____

Categories   1. _____
           2. _____

Keywords   1. _____
          2. _____
          3. _____
          4. _____
          5. _____
          6. _____
          7. _____

Book _____

Description _____

_____

Book Cover _____

Date First Sale ___/___/___ =   Q1   Q2   Q3   Q4
                ☐ Unpublished on ___/___/___

30   **Title Details**

Title   _____

Subtitle   _____

ISBN   _____ - _____

Book Type   ☐ eBook   ☐ Paperback

          ☐ Hardcover   ☐ Audiobook

          ☐ Shareable PDF

Version   _____ Edition _____

Series   _____

Page Count   _____ Trim Size _____ x _____

Date Published   ____/____/____   =   Q1   Q2   Q3   Q4

Publisher   ☐ KDP   ☐ KDP Print   ☐ IngramSpark

Account(s)   ☐ _____   ☐ _____

          ☐ _____   ☐ _____

Price $_____ Currency _____

Markets   ☐ Global   ☐ _____   ☐ _____

          ☐ _____   ☐ _____   ☐ _____

Categories   1. _____

          2. _____

Keywords   1. _____

          2. _____

          3. _____

          4. _____

          5. _____

          6. _____

          7. _____

Book Description   _____

          _____

          _____

Book Cover   _____

Date First Sale   ____/____/____   =   Q1   Q2   Q3   Q4

          ☐ Unpublished on ____/____/____

Title Details

Title _____

Subtitle _____

ISBN _____ - _____

Book Type   ☐ eBook   ☐ Paperback
             ☐ Hardcover   ☐ Audiobook
             ☐ Shareable PDF

Version _____   Edition _____

Series _____

Page Count _____   Trim Size _____ x _____

Date Published ____/____/____ = Q1   Q2   Q3   Q4

Publisher   ☐ KDP   ☐ KDP Print   ☐ IngramSpark

Account(s)   ☐ _____   ☐ _____
             ☐ _____   ☐ _____

Price $_____   Currency _____

Markets   ☐ Global   ☐ _____   ☐ _____
             ☐ _____   ☐ _____   ☐ _____

Categories   1. _____
             2. _____

Keywords   1. _____
             2. _____
             3. _____
             4. _____
             5. _____
             6. _____
             7. _____

Book
Description _____
             _____
             _____

Book Cover   _____

Date First Sale ____/____/____ = Q1   Q2   Q3   Q4
                        ☐ Unpublished on ____/____/____

32

Title Details

Title _____

Subtitle _____

ISBN _____ - _____

Book Type
☐ eBook ☐ Paperback
☐ Hardcover ☐ Audiobook
☐ Shareable PDF

Version _____ Edition _____

Series _____

Page Count _____ Trim Size _____ x _____

Date Published ____/____/____ = Q1 Q2 Q3 Q4

Publisher ☐ KDP ☐ KDP Print ☐ IngramSpark

Account(s) ☐ _____ ☐ _____
☐ _____ ☐ _____

Price $_____ Currency _____

Markets ☐ Global ☐ _____ ☐ _____
☐ _____ ☐ _____ ☐ _____

Categories
1. _____
2. _____

Keywords
1. _____
2. _____
3. _____
4. _____
5. _____
6. _____
7. _____

Book Description _____
_____
_____

Book Cover _____

Date First Sale ____/____/____ = Q1 Q2 Q3 Q4
☐ Unpublished on ____/____/____

Title Details

Title _____

Subtitle _____

ISBN _____ - _____

Book Type □ eBook   □ Paperback
           □ Hardcover   □ Audiobook
           □ Shareable PDF

Version _____ Edition _____

Series _____

Page Count _____ Trim Size _____ x _____

Date Published ____/____/____ = Q1   Q2   Q3   Q4

Publisher □ KDP □ KDP Print   □ IngramSpark

Account(s) □ _____   □ _____
            □ _____   □ _____

Price $_____ Currency _____

Markets □ Global   □ _____   □ _____
         □ _____ □ _____   □ _____

Categories 1. _____
            2. _____

Keywords 1. _____
          2. _____
          3. _____
          4. _____
          5. _____
          6. _____
          7. _____

Book
Description _____
           _____
           _____

Book Cover _____

Date First Sale ____/____/____ = Q1   Q2   Q3   Q4
                □ Unpublished on ____/____/____

34

Title Details

Title _____

Subtitle _____

ISBN _____ - _____

Book Type   □ eBook   □ Paperback
              □ Hardcover   □ Audiobook
              □ Shareable PDF

Version _____ Edition _____

Series _____

Page Count _____ Trim Size _____ x _____

Date Published ____/____/____ =   Q1   Q2   Q3   Q4

Publisher   □ KDP   □ KDP Print   □ IngramSpark

Account(s)   □ _____   □ _____
          □ _____   □ _____

Price $_____ Currency _____

Markets   □ Global   □ _____   □ _____
        □ _____   □ _____   □ _____

Categories   1. _____
          2. _____

Keywords   1. _____
         2. _____
         3. _____
         4. _____
         5. _____
         6. _____
         7. _____

Book _____

Description _____
_____

Book Cover _____

Date First Sale   ____/____/____ =   Q1   Q2   Q3   Q4
                  □ Unpublished on ____/____/____

Title Details **35**

Title   _____

Subtitle   _____

ISBN   _____ - _____

Book Type   ☐ eBook   ☐ Paperback

                  ☐ Hardcover   ☐ Audiobook

                  ☐ Shareable PDF

Version   _____   Edition   _____

Series   _____

Page Count   _____   Trim Size   _____ x _____

Date Published   ____/____/____   =   Q1   Q2   Q3   Q4

Publisher   ☐ KDP   ☐ KDP Print   ☐ IngramSpark

Account(s)   ☐ _____   ☐ _____

                ☐ _____   ☐ _____

Price $_____   Currency _____

Markets   ☐ Global   ☐ _____   ☐ _____

         ☐ _____   ☐ _____   ☐ _____

Categories   1. _____

                2. _____

Keywords   1. _____

                2. _____

                3. _____

                4. _____

                5. _____

                6. _____

                7. _____

Book   _____

Description   _____

                _____

Book Cover   _____

Date First Sale   ____/____/____   =   Q1   Q2   Q3   Q4

                               ☐ Unpublished on ____/____/____

36 **Title Details**

Title _____

Subtitle _____

ISBN _____ - _____

Book Type   ☐ eBook   ☐ Paperback
         ☐ Hardcover   ☐ Audiobook
         ☐ Shareable PDF

Version _____ Edition _____

Series _____

Page Count _____ Trim Size _____ x _____

Date Published ____/____/____ = Q1   Q2   Q3   Q4

Publisher   ☐ KDP   ☐ KDP Print   ☐ IngramSpark

Account(s)   ☐ _____   ☐ _____
         ☐ _____   ☐ _____

Price $_____ Currency _____

Markets   ☐ Global   ☐ _____   ☐ _____
         ☐ _____   ☐ _____   ☐ _____

Categories   1. _____
2. _____

Keywords   1. _____
2. _____
3. _____
4. _____
5. _____
6. _____
7. _____

Book Description _____

_____

_____

Book Cover _____

Date First Sale ____/____/____ = Q1   Q2   Q3   Q4
         ☐ Unpublished on ____/____/____

Title Details **37**

Title _____

Subtitle _____

ISBN _____ - _____

Book Type
☐ eBook ☐ Paperback
☐ Hardcover ☐ Audiobook
☐ Shareable PDF

Version _____ Edition _____

Series _____

Page Count _____ Trim Size _____ x _____

Date Published ____/____/____ = Q1 Q2 Q3 Q4

Publisher ☐ KDP ☐ KDP Print ☐ IngramSpark

Account(s)
☐ _____ ☐ _____
☐ _____ ☐ _____

Price $_____ Currency _____

Markets
☐ Global ☐ _____ ☐ _____
☐ _____ ☐ _____ ☐ _____

Categories
1. _____
2. _____

Keywords
1. _____
2. _____
3. _____
4. _____
5. _____
6. _____
7. _____

Book
Description _____
_____
_____

Book Cover _____

Date First Sale ____/____/____ = Q1 Q2 Q3 Q4
☐ Unpublished on ____/____/____

38   **Title Details**

Title _____

Subtitle _____

ISBN _____ - _____

Book Type
☐ eBook ☐ Paperback
☐ Hardcover ☐ Audiobook
☐ Shareable PDF

Version _____ Edition _____

Series _____

Page Count _____ Trim Size _____ x _____

Date Published ___/___/___ = Q1 Q2 Q3 Q4

Publisher ☐ KDP ☐ KDP Print ☐ IngramSpark

Account(s) ☐ _____ ☐ _____
☐ _____ ☐ _____

Price $_____ Currency _____

Markets ☐ Global ☐ _____ ☐ _____
☐ _____ ☐ _____ ☐ _____

Categories
1. _____
2. _____

Keywords
1. _____
2. _____
3. _____
4. _____
5. _____
6. _____
7. _____

Book Description _____
_____
_____

Book Cover _____

Date First Sale ___/___/___ = Q1 Q2 Q3 Q4
☐ Unpublished on ___/___/___

Title Details

Title _____

Subtitle _____

ISBN _____ - _____

Book Type   □ eBook   □ Paperback

               □ Hardcover   □ Audiobook

               □ Shareable PDF

Version   _____   Edition   _____

Series _____

Page Count   _____   Trim Size   _____ x _____

Date Published   ____/____/____   =   Q1   Q2   Q3   Q4

Publisher   □ KDP   □ KDP Print   □ IngramSpark

Account(s)   □ _____   □ _____

             □ _____   □ _____

Price $_____   Currency _____

Markets   □ Global   □ _____   □ _____

        □ _____   □ _____   □ _____

Categories   1. _____

            2. _____

Keywords   1. _____

           2. _____

           3. _____

           4. _____

           5. _____

           6. _____

           7. _____

Book _____

Description _____

_____

Book Cover _____

Date First Sale   ____/____/____   =   Q1   Q2   Q3   Q4

                                  □ Unpublished on ____/____/____

40 **Title Details**

Title _____

Subtitle _____

ISBN _____ - _____

Book Type ☐ eBook ☐ Paperback
☐ Hardcover ☐ Audiobook
☐ Shareable PDF

Version _____ Edition _____

Series _____

Page Count _____ Trim Size _____ x _____

Date Published ____/____/____ = Q1 Q2 Q3 Q4

Publisher ☐ KDP ☐ KDP Print ☐ IngramSpark

Account(s) ☐ _____ ☐ _____
☐ _____ ☐ _____

Price $_____ Currency _____

Markets ☐ Global ☐ _____ ☐ _____
☐ _____ ☐ _____ ☐ _____

Categories 1. _____
2. _____

Keywords 1. _____
2. _____
3. _____
4. _____
5. _____
6. _____
7. _____

Book _____
Description _____
_____

Book Cover _____

Date First Sale ____/____/____ = Q1 Q2 Q3 Q4
☐ Unpublished on ____/____/____

Title Details

Title _____

Subtitle _____

ISBN _____ - _____

Book Type   ☐ eBook   ☐ Paperback

☐ Hardcover   ☐ Audiobook

☐ Shareable PDF

Version _____ Edition _____

Series _____

Page Count _____ Trim Size _____ x _____

Date Published ____/____/____ = Q1   Q2   Q3   Q4

Publisher   ☐ KDP ☐ KDP Print   ☐ IngramSpark

Account(s)   ☐ _____   ☐ _____

☐ _____   ☐ _____

Price $_____ Currency _____

Markets   ☐ Global   ☐ _____   ☐ _____

☐ _____   ☐ _____   ☐ _____

Categories   1. _____

2. _____

Keywords   1. _____

2. _____

3. _____

4. _____

5. _____

6. _____

7. _____

Book   _____

Description   _____

_____

Book Cover   _____

Date First Sale   ____/____/____ = Q1   Q2   Q3   Q4

☐ Unpublished on ____/____/____

42

Title Details

Title   _____

Subtitle   _____

ISBN   _____ - _____

Book Type   ☐ eBook   ☐ Paperback

                  ☐ Hardcover   ☐ Audiobook

                  ☐ Shareable PDF

Version   _____ Edition   _____

Series   _____

Page Count   _____ Trim Size   _____ x _____

Date Published   ____/____/____   =   Q1   Q2   Q3   Q4

Publisher   ☐ KDP   ☐ KDP Print   ☐ IngramSpark

Account(s)   ☐ _____   ☐ _____

               ☐ _____   ☐ _____

Price $_____   Currency _____

Markets   ☐ Global   ☐ _____   ☐ _____

           ☐ _____   ☐ _____   ☐ _____

Categories   1. _____

            2. _____

Keywords   1. _____

            2. _____

            3. _____

            4. _____

            5. _____

            6. _____

            7. _____

Book   _____

Description   _____

             _____

             _____

Book Cover   _____

Date First Sale   ____/____/____   =   Q1   Q2   Q3   Q4

                               ☐ Unpublished on ____/____/____

Title Details   **43**

Title _____

Subtitle _____

ISBN _____ - _____

Book Type   □ eBook   □ Paperback
            □ Hardcover   □ Audiobook
            □ Shareable PDF

Version _____ Edition _____

Series _____

Page Count _____ Trim Size _____ x _____

Date Published ___/___/___ = Q1   Q2   Q3   Q4

Publisher   □ KDP   □ KDP Print   □ IngramSpark

Account(s)   □ _____   □ _____
          □ _____   □ _____

Price $_____ Currency _____

Markets   □ Global   □ _____   □ _____
       □ _____   □ _____   □ _____

Categories
1. _____
2. _____

Keywords
1. _____
2. _____
3. _____
4. _____
5. _____
6. _____
7. _____

Book Description _____
_____
_____

Book Cover _____

Date First Sale ___/___/___ = Q1   Q2   Q3   Q4
           □ Unpublished on ___/___/___

44

Title Details

Title	_____
Subtitle	_____
ISBN	_____ - _____
Book Type	☐ eBook ☐ Paperback
	☐ Hardcover ☐ Audiobook
	☐ Shareable PDF
Version	_____ Edition _____
Series	_____
Page Count	_____ Trim Size _____ x _____
Date Published	____/____/____ = Q1 Q2 Q3 Q4
Publisher	☐ KDP ☐ KDP Print ☐ IngramSpark
Account(s)	☐ _____ ☐ _____
	☐ _____ ☐ _____
Price	$_____ Currency _____
Markets	☐ Global ☐ _____ ☐ _____
	☐ _____ ☐ _____ ☐ _____
Categories	1. _____
	2. _____
Keywords	1. _____
	2. _____
	3. _____
	4. _____
	5. _____
	6. _____
	7. _____
Book Description	_____
	_____
	_____
Book Cover	_____
Date First Sale	____/____/____ = Q1 Q2 Q3 Q4
	☐ Unpublished on ____/____/____

Title Details

Title _____

Subtitle _____

ISBN _____ - _____

Book Type
☐ eBook   ☐ Paperback
☐ Hardcover   ☐ Audiobook
☐ Shareable PDF

Version _____ Edition _____

Series _____

Page Count _____ Trim Size _____ x _____

Date Published ____/____/____ = Q1 Q2 Q3 Q4

Publisher ☐ KDP ☐ KDP Print ☐ IngramSpark

Account(s)
☐ _____   ☐ _____
☐ _____   ☐ _____

Price $_____ Currency _____

Markets
☐ Global   ☐ _____   ☐ _____
☐ _____   ☐ _____   ☐ _____

Categories
1. _____
2. _____

Keywords
1. _____
2. _____
3. _____
4. _____
5. _____
6. _____
7. _____

Book Description _____
_____
_____

Book Cover _____

Date First Sale ____/____/____ = Q1 Q2 Q3 Q4
☐ Unpublished on ____/____/____

46

Title Details

Title _____

Subtitle _____

ISBN _____ - _____

Book Type
☐ eBook ☐ Paperback
☐ Hardcover ☐ Audiobook
☐ Shareable PDF

Version _____ Edition _____

Series _____

Page Count _____ Trim Size _____ x _____

Date Published ____/____/____ = | Q1 | Q2 | Q3 | Q4 |

Publisher ☐ KDP ☐ KDP Print ☐ IngramSpark

Account(s)
☐ _____ ☐ _____
☐ _____ ☐ _____

Price $_____ Currency _____

Markets
☐ Global ☐ _____ ☐ _____
☐ _____ ☐ _____ ☐ _____

Categories
1. _____
2. _____

Keywords
1. _____
2. _____
3. _____
4. _____
5. _____
6. _____
7. _____

Book
Description _____
_____
_____

Book Cover _____

Date First Sale ____/____/____ = | Q1 | Q2 | Q3 | Q4 |

☐ Unpublished on ____/____/____

Title Details

Title _____

Subtitle _____

ISBN _____ - _____

Book Type ☐ eBook   ☐ Paperback
           ☐ Hardcover   ☐ Audiobook
           ☐ Shareable PDF

Version _____ Edition _____

Series _____

Page Count _____ Trim Size _____ x _____

Date Published ____/____/____ = Q1   Q2   Q3   Q4

Publisher ☐ KDP ☐ KDP Print   ☐ IngramSpark

Account(s) ☐ _____   ☐ _____
            ☐ _____   ☐ _____

Price $_____ Currency _____

Markets ☐ Global   ☐ _____   ☐ _____
         ☐ _____   ☐ _____   ☐ _____

Categories 1. _____
            2. _____

Keywords 1. _____
          2. _____
          3. _____
          4. _____
          5. _____
          6. _____
          7. _____

Book Description _____
_____
_____

Book Cover _____

Date First Sale ____/____/____ = Q1   Q2   Q3   Q4

☐ Unpublished on ____/____/____

48

Title Details

Title _____

Subtitle _____

ISBN _____ - _____

Book Type
- ☐ eBook ☐ Paperback
- ☐ Hardcover ☐ Audiobook
- ☐ Shareable PDF

Version _____ Edition _____

Series _____

Page Count _____ Trim Size _____ x _____

Date Published ____/____/____ = Q1 Q2 Q3 Q4

Publisher ☐ KDP ☐ KDP Print ☐ IngramSpark

Account(s)
- ☐ _____ ☐ _____
- ☐ _____ ☐ _____

Price $_____ Currency _____

Markets
- ☐ Global ☐ _____ ☐ _____
- ☐ _____ ☐ _____ ☐ _____

Categories
1. _____
2. _____

Keywords
1. _____
2. _____
3. _____
4. _____
5. _____
6. _____
7. _____

Book
Description _____
_____
_____

Book Cover _____

Date First Sale ____/____/____ = Q1 Q2 Q3 Q4

☐ Unpublished on ____/____/____

Title Details   **49**

Title   _____

Subtitle   _____

ISBN   _____ - _____

Book Type
- ☐ eBook   ☐ Paperback
- ☐ Hardcover   ☐ Audiobook
- ☐ Shareable PDF

Version   _____   Edition   _____

Series   _____

Page Count   _____   Trim Size   _____ x _____

Date Published   ____/____/____   =   Q1   Q2   Q3   Q4

Publisher   ☐ KDP   ☐ KDP Print   ☐ IngramSpark

Account(s)
- ☐ _____   ☐ _____
- ☐ _____   ☐ _____

Price $_____   Currency _____

Markets
- ☐ Global   ☐ _____   ☐ _____
- ☐ _____   ☐ _____   ☐ _____

Categories
1. _____
2. _____

Keywords
1. _____
2. _____
3. _____
4. _____
5. _____
6. _____
7. _____

Book Description   _____
_____
_____

Book Cover   _____

Date First Sale   ____/____/____   =   Q1   Q2   Q3   Q4

☐ Unpublished on ____/____/____

50

Title Details

Title _____

Subtitle _____

ISBN _____ - _____

Book Type ☐ eBook   ☐ Paperback
            ☐ Hardcover   ☐ Audiobook
            ☐ Shareable PDF

Version _____ Edition _____

Series _____

Page Count _____ Trim Size _____ x _____

Date Published ____/____/____ =   Q1   Q2   Q3   Q4

Publisher ☐ KDP ☐ KDP Print   ☐ IngramSpark

Account(s) ☐ _____   ☐ _____
            ☐ _____   ☐ _____

Price $_____ Currency _____

Markets ☐ Global   ☐ _____   ☐ _____
            ☐ _____   ☐ _____   ☐ _____

Categories 1. _____
            2. _____

Keywords 1. _____
            2. _____
            3. _____
            4. _____
            5. _____
            6. _____
            7. _____

Book _____

Description _____

_____

Book Cover _____

Date First Sale ____/____/____ =   Q1   Q2   Q3   Q4
            ☐ Unpublished on ____/____/____

Title Details

Title _____

Subtitle _____

ISBN _____ - _____

Book Type
☐ eBook   ☐ Paperback
☐ Hardcover   ☐ Audiobook
☐ Shareable PDF

Version _____ Edition _____

Series _____

Page Count _____ Trim Size _____ x _____

Date Published ____/____/____   =   Q1   Q2   Q3   Q4

Publisher ☐ KDP   ☐ KDP Print   ☐ IngramSpark

Account(s)
☐ _____   ☐ _____
☐ _____   ☐ _____

Price $_____ Currency _____

Markets
☐ Global   ☐ _____   ☐ _____
☐ _____   ☐ _____   ☐ _____

Categories
1. _____
2. _____

Keywords
1. _____
2. _____
3. _____
4. _____
5. _____
6. _____
7. _____

Book Description
_____
_____
_____

Book Cover _____

Date First Sale ____/____/____   =   Q1   Q2   Q3   Q4
☐ Unpublished on ____/____/____

52

Title Details

Title   _____

Subtitle   _____

ISBN   _____ - _____

Book Type   ☐ eBook   ☐ Paperback
               ☐ Hardcover   ☐ Audiobook
               ☐ Shareable PDF

Version   _____ Edition _____

Series   _____

Page Count   _____ Trim Size _____ x _____

Date Published ____/____/____ = Q1   Q2   Q3   Q4

Publisher   ☐ KDP   ☐ KDP Print   ☐ IngramSpark

Account(s)   ☐ _____   ☐ _____
               ☐ _____   ☐ _____

Price $_____ Currency _____

Markets   ☐ Global   ☐ _____   ☐ _____
               ☐ _____   ☐ _____   ☐ _____

Categories   1. _____
               2. _____

Keywords   1. _____
               2. _____
               3. _____
               4. _____
               5. _____
               6. _____
               7. _____

Book   _____
Description   _____
               _____
               _____

Book Cover   _____

Date First Sale ____/____/____ = Q1   Q2   Q3   Q4
                          ☐ Unpublished on ____/____/____

Title Details **53**

Title   _____

Subtitle   _____

ISBN   _____ - _____

Book Type   ☐ eBook   ☐ Paperback
            ☐ Hardcover   ☐ Audiobook
            ☐ Shareable PDF

Version   _____   Edition   _____

Series   _____

Page Count   _____   Trim Size   _____ x _____

Date Published   _____/_____/_____   =   Q1   Q2   Q3   Q4

Publisher   ☐ KDP   ☐ KDP Print   ☐ IngramSpark

Account(s)   ☐ _____   ☐ _____
            ☐ _____   ☐ _____

Price $_____   Currency _____

Markets   ☐ Global   ☐ _____   ☐ _____
            ☐ _____   ☐ _____   ☐ _____

Categories   1. _____
            2. _____

Keywords   1. _____
            2. _____
            3. _____
            4. _____
            5. _____
            6. _____
            7. _____

Book   _____

Description   _____
            _____

Book Cover   _____

Date First Sale   _____/_____/_____   =   Q1   Q2   Q3   Q4
            ☐ Unpublished on _____/_____/_____

54   **Title Details**

Title   _____
Subtitle   _____
ISBN   _____ - _____
Book Type   ☐ eBook   ☐ Paperback
                    ☐ Hardcover   ☐ Audiobook
                    ☐ Shareable PDF
Version   _____ Edition _____
Series   _____
Page Count   _____ Trim Size _____ x _____
Date Published   ____/____/____   =   Q1   Q2   Q3   Q4
Publisher   ☐ KDP   ☐ KDP Print   ☐ IngramSpark
Account(s)   ☐ _____   ☐ _____
                    ☐ _____   ☐ _____
Price $_____ Currency _____
Markets   ☐ Global   ☐ _____   ☐ _____
                    ☐ _____   ☐ _____   ☐ _____
Categories   1. _____
                    2. _____
Keywords   1. _____
                    2. _____
                    3. _____
                    4. _____
                    5. _____
                    6. _____
                    7. _____
Book   _____
Description   _____
                    _____
Book Cover   _____
Date First Sale   ____/____/____   =   Q1   Q2   Q3   Q4
                          ☐ Unpublished on ____/____/____

Title Details **55**

Title _____

Subtitle _____

ISBN _____ - _____

Book Type ☐ eBook ☐ Paperback
☐ Hardcover ☐ Audiobook
☐ Shareable PDF

Version _____ Edition _____

Series _____

Page Count _____ Trim Size _____ x _____

Date Published ____/____/____ = Q1 Q2 Q3 Q4

Publisher ☐ KDP ☐ KDP Print ☐ IngramSpark

Account(s) ☐ _____ ☐ _____
☐ _____ ☐ _____

Price $_____ Currency _____

Markets ☐ Global ☐ _____ ☐ _____
☐ _____ ☐ _____ ☐ _____

Categories 1. _____
2. _____

Keywords 1. _____
2. _____
3. _____
4. _____
5. _____
6. _____
7. _____

Book _____
Description _____
_____

Book Cover _____

Date First Sale ____/____/____ = Q1 Q2 Q3 Q4
☐ Unpublished on ____/____/____

56

Title Details

Title   _____

Subtitle   _____

ISBN   _____ - _____

Book Type   ☐ eBook   ☐ Paperback
                 ☐ Hardcover   ☐ Audiobook
                 ☐ Shareable PDF

Version   _____ Edition _____

Series   _____

Page Count   _____ Trim Size   _____ x _____

Date Published   ____/____/____ =   Q1   Q2   Q3   Q4

Publisher   ☐ KDP ☐ KDP Print   ☐ IngramSpark

Account(s)   ☐ _____   ☐ _____
                 ☐ _____   ☐ _____

Price $_____ Currency _____

Markets   ☐ Global   ☐ _____   ☐ _____
                 ☐ _____ ☐ _____   ☐ _____

Categories   1. _____
                 2. _____

Keywords   1. _____
                 2. _____
                 3. _____
                 4. _____
                 5. _____
                 6. _____
                 7. _____

Book   _____
Description   _____
                 _____
                 _____

Book Cover   _____

Date First Sale ____/____/____   =   Q1   Q2   Q3   Q4
                                  ☐ Unpublished on ____/____/____

Title Details   **57**

Title _____

Subtitle _____

ISBN _____ - _____

Book Type
☐ eBook   ☐ Paperback
☐ Hardcover   ☐ Audiobook
☐ Shareable PDF

Version _____ Edition _____

Series _____

Page Count _____ Trim Size _____ x _____

Date Published ____/____/____ = Q1   Q2   Q3   Q4

Publisher ☐ KDP ☐ KDP Print ☐ IngramSpark

Account(s)
☐ _____   ☐ _____
☐ _____   ☐ _____

Price $_____ Currency _____

Markets
☐ Global   ☐ _____   ☐ _____
☐ _____   ☐ _____   ☐ _____

Categories
1. _____
2. _____

Keywords
1. _____
2. _____
3. _____
4. _____
5. _____
6. _____
7. _____

Book
Description
_____
_____
_____

Book Cover _____

Date First Sale ____/____/____ = Q1   Q2   Q3   Q4
☐ Unpublished on ____/____/____

58

Title Details

Title _____

Subtitle _____

ISBN _____ - _____

Book Type   □ eBook   □ Paperback
            □ Hardcover   □ Audiobook
            □ Shareable PDF

Version _____ Edition _____

Series _____

Page Count _____ Trim Size _____ x _____

Date Published ____/____/____   =   Q1   Q2   Q3   Q4

Publisher   □ KDP   □ KDP Print   □ IngramSpark

Account(s)   □ _____   □ _____
            □ _____   □ _____

Price $_____ Currency _____

Markets   □ Global   □ _____   □ _____
            □ _____   □ _____   □ _____

Categories   1. _____
            2. _____

Keywords   1. _____
            2. _____
            3. _____
            4. _____
            5. _____
            6. _____
            7. _____

Book _____

Description _____

_____

_____

Book Cover _____

Date First Sale ____/____/____   =   Q1   Q2   Q3   Q4

            □ Unpublished on ____/____/____

Title Details

Title _____

Subtitle _____

ISBN _____ - _____

Book Type   ☐ eBook   ☐ Paperback

               ☐ Hardcover   ☐ Audiobook

               ☐ Shareable PDF

Version _____   Edition _____

Series _____

Page Count _____   Trim Size _____ x _____

Date Published ____/____/____   =   Q1   Q2   Q3   Q4

Publisher   ☐ KDP   ☐ KDP Print   ☐ IngramSpark

Account(s)   ☐ _____   ☐ _____

               ☐ _____   ☐ _____

Price $_____   Currency _____

Markets   ☐ Global   ☐ _____   ☐ _____

               ☐ _____   ☐ _____   ☐ _____

Categories   1. _____

               2. _____

Keywords   1. _____

               2. _____

               3. _____

               4. _____

               5. _____

               6. _____

               7. _____

Book _____

Description _____

_____

Book Cover _____

Date First Sale ____/____/____   =   Q1   Q2   Q3   Q4

                              ☐ Unpublished on ____/____/____

60

Title Details

Title _____

Subtitle _____

ISBN _____ - _____

Book Type
- ☐ eBook
- ☐ Hardcover
- ☐ Shareable PDF
- ☐ Paperback
- ☐ Audiobook

Version _____ Edition _____

Series _____

Page Count _____ Trim Size _____ x _____

Date Published ____/____/____ = Q1   Q2   Q3   Q4

Publisher ☐ KDP ☐ KDP Print   ☐ IngramSpark

Account(s)
- ☐ _____
- ☐ _____
- ☐ _____
- ☐ _____

Price $_____ Currency _____

Markets
- ☐ Global
- ☐ _____   ☐ _____
- ☐ _____   ☐ _____   ☐ _____

Categories
1. _____
2. _____

Keywords
1. _____
2. _____
3. _____
4. _____
5. _____
6. _____
7. _____

Book Description _____
_____
_____
_____

Book Cover _____

Date First Sale ____/____/____ = Q1   Q2   Q3   Q4

☐ Unpublished on ____/____/____

Title Details

Title _____

Subtitle _____

ISBN _____ - _____

Book Type
☐ eBook ☐ Paperback
☐ Hardcover ☐ Audiobook
☐ Shareable PDF

Version _____ Edition _____

Series _____

Page Count _____ Trim Size _____ x _____

Date Published ____/____/____ = Q1 Q2 Q3 Q4

Publisher ☐ KDP ☐ KDP Print ☐ IngramSpark

Account(s)
☐ _____ ☐ _____
☐ _____ ☐ _____

Price $_____ Currency _____

Markets
☐ Global ☐ _____ ☐ _____
☐ _____ ☐ _____ ☐ _____

Categories
1. _____
2. _____

Keywords
1. _____
2. _____
3. _____
4. _____
5. _____
6. _____
7. _____

Book _____

Description _____
_____

Book Cover _____

Date First Sale ____/____/____ = Q1 Q2 Q3 Q4
☐ Unpublished on ____/____/____

62   **Title Details**

Title   _____

Subtitle   _____

ISBN   _____ - _____

Book Type   ☐ eBook   ☐ Paperback
             ☐ Hardcover   ☐ Audiobook
             ☐ Shareable PDF

Version   _____   Edition _____

Series   _____

Page Count   _____   Trim Size   _____ x _____

Date Published ____/____/____ = Q1   Q2   Q3   Q4

Publisher   ☐ KDP ☐ KDP Print   ☐ IngramSpark

Account(s)   ☐ _____   ☐ _____
             ☐ _____   ☐ _____

Price $_____   Currency _____

Markets   ☐ Global   ☐ _____   ☐ _____
             ☐ _____   ☐ _____   ☐ _____

Categories   1. _____
             2. _____

Keywords   1. _____
             2. _____
             3. _____
             4. _____
             5. _____
             6. _____
             7. _____

Book   _____
Description _____
             _____

Book Cover   _____

Date First Sale ____/____/____ = Q1   Q2   Q3   Q4
             ☐ Unpublished on ____/____/____

Title Details

Title _____

Subtitle _____

ISBN _____ - _____

Book Type ☐ eBook ☐ Paperback
☐ Hardcover ☐ Audiobook
☐ Shareable PDF

Version _____ Edition _____

Series _____

Page Count _____ Trim Size _____ x _____

Date Published ____/____/____ = Q1 Q2 Q3 Q4

Publisher ☐ KDP ☐ KDP Print ☐ IngramSpark

Account(s) ☐ _____ ☐ _____
☐ _____ ☐ _____

Price $_____ Currency _____

Markets ☐ Global ☐ _____ ☐ _____
☐ _____ ☐ _____ ☐ _____

Categories 1. _____
2. _____

Keywords 1. _____
2. _____
3. _____
4. _____
5. _____
6. _____
7. _____

Book _____

Description _____

_____

Book Cover _____

Date First Sale ____/____/____ = Q1 Q2 Q3 Q4
☐ Unpublished on ____/____/____

64

Title Details

Title   _____

Subtitle   _____

ISBN   _____ - _____

Book Type   ☐ eBook   ☐ Paperback
               ☐ Hardcover   ☐ Audiobook
               ☐ Shareable PDF

Version   _____ Edition _____

Series   _____

Page Count   _____ Trim Size _____ x _____

Date Published ____/____/____ = | Q1 | Q2 | Q3 | Q4 |

Publisher   ☐ KDP   ☐ KDP Print   ☐ IngramSpark

Account(s)   ☐ _____   ☐ _____
               ☐ _____   ☐ _____

Price $_____ Currency _____

Markets   ☐ Global   ☐ _____   ☐ _____
               ☐ _____   ☐ _____   ☐ _____

Categories   1. _____
               2. _____

Keywords   1. _____
               2. _____
               3. _____
               4. _____
               5. _____
               6. _____
               7. _____

Book   _____
Description   _____
               _____

Book Cover   _____

Date First Sale ____/____/____ = | Q1 | Q2 | Q3 | Q4 |

               ☐ Unpublished on ____/____/____

Title Details

Title _____

Subtitle _____

ISBN _____ - _____

Book Type ☐ eBook   ☐ Paperback
           ☐ Hardcover   ☐ Audiobook
           ☐ Shareable PDF

Version _____ Edition _____

Series _____

Page Count _____ Trim Size _____ x _____

Date Published ____/____/____ = Q1   Q2   Q3   Q4

Publisher ☐ KDP ☐ KDP Print   ☐ IngramSpark

Account(s) ☐ _____   ☐ _____
            ☐ _____   ☐ _____

Price $_____ Currency _____

Markets ☐ Global   ☐ _____   ☐ _____
         ☐ _____ ☐ _____   ☐ _____

Categories 1. _____
            2. _____

Keywords 1. _____
          2. _____
          3. _____
          4. _____
          5. _____
          6. _____
          7. _____

Book
Description _____
            _____
            _____

Book Cover _____

Date First Sale ____/____/____ = Q1   Q2   Q3   Q4
                        ☐ Unpublished on ____/____/____

66

Title Details

Title _____

Subtitle _____

ISBN _____ - _____

Book Type   ☐ eBook   ☐ Paperback
                   ☐ Hardcover   ☐ Audiobook
                   ☐ Shareable PDF

Version   _____ Edition _____

Series _____

Page Count   _____ Trim Size   _____ x _____

Date Published   ____/____/____ =   Q1   Q2   Q3   Q4

Publisher   ☐ KDP   ☐ KDP Print   ☐ IngramSpark

Account(s)   ☐ _____   ☐ _____
                ☐ _____   ☐ _____

Price $_____ Currency _____

Markets   ☐ Global   ☐ _____   ☐ _____
         ☐ _____   ☐ _____   ☐ _____

Categories   1. _____
           2. _____

Keywords   1. _____
           2. _____
           3. _____
           4. _____
           5. _____
           6. _____
           7. _____

Book _____

Description _____
_____

Book Cover _____

Date First Sale   ____/____/____ =   Q1   Q2   Q3   Q4
                            ☐ Unpublished on ____/____/____

Title Details

Title _____

Subtitle _____

ISBN _____ - _____

Book Type □ eBook   □ Paperback

      □ Hardcover   □ Audiobook

      □ Shareable PDF

Version _____ Edition _____

Series _____

Page Count _____ Trim Size _____ x _____

Date Published _____/_____/_____ = Q1   Q2   Q3   Q4

Publisher □ KDP   □ KDP Print   □ IngramSpark

Account(s) □ _____   □ _____

     □ _____   □ _____

Price $_____ Currency _____

Markets □ Global   □ _____   □ _____

    □ _____   □ _____   □ _____

Categories 1. _____

      2. _____

Keywords 1. _____

      2. _____

      3. _____

      4. _____

      5. _____

      6. _____

      7. _____

Book _____

Description _____

      _____

Book Cover _____

Date First Sale _____/_____/_____ = Q1   Q2   Q3   Q4

           □ Unpublished on _____/_____/_____

68

Title Details

Title _____

Subtitle _____

ISBN _____ - _____

Book Type   ☐ eBook   ☐ Paperback

              ☐ Hardcover   ☐ Audiobook

              ☐ Shareable PDF

Version _____ Edition _____

Series _____

Page Count _____ Trim Size _____ x _____

Date Published ____/____/____ =   Q1   Q2   Q3   Q4

Publisher   ☐ KDP   ☐ KDP Print   ☐ IngramSpark

Account(s)   ☐ _____   ☐ _____

            ☐ _____   ☐ _____

Price $_____   Currency _____

Markets   ☐ Global   ☐ _____   ☐ _____

        ☐ _____   ☐ _____   ☐ _____

Categories   1. _____

            2. _____

Keywords   1. _____

            2. _____

            3. _____

            4. _____

            5. _____

            6. _____

            7. _____

Book _____

Description _____

_____

Book Cover _____

Date First Sale   ____/____/____   =   Q1   Q2   Q3   Q4

                           ☐ Unpublished on ____/____/____

Title Details

Title _____

Subtitle _____

ISBN _____ - _____

Book Type   ☐ eBook   ☐ Paperback

              ☐ Hardcover   ☐ Audiobook

              ☐ Shareable PDF

Version _____ Edition _____

Series _____

Page Count _____ Trim Size _____ x _____

Date Published ____/____/____   =   Q1   Q2   Q3   Q4

Publisher   ☐ KDP   ☐ KDP Print   ☐ IngramSpark

Account(s)   ☐ _____   ☐ _____

           ☐ _____   ☐ _____

Price $_____   Currency _____

Markets   ☐ Global   ☐ _____   ☐ _____

        ☐ _____   ☐ _____   ☐ _____

Categories   1. _____

           2. _____

Keywords   1. _____

           2. _____

           3. _____

           4. _____

           5. _____

           6. _____

           7. _____

Book _____

Description _____

           _____

Book Cover _____

Date First Sale ____/____/____   =   Q1   Q2   Q3   Q4

                            ☐ Unpublished on ____/____/____

70

Title Details

Title   _____
Subtitle   _____
ISBN   _____ - _____
Book Type   ☐ eBook   ☐ Paperback
               ☐ Hardcover   ☐ Audiobook
               ☐ Shareable PDF
Version   _____ Edition   _____
Series   _____
Page Count   _____ Trim Size   _____ x _____
Date Published ____/____/____   =   Q1   Q2   Q3   Q4
Publisher   ☐ KDP   ☐ KDP Print   ☐ IngramSpark
Account(s)   ☐ _____   ☐ _____
               ☐ _____   ☐ _____
Price $_____ Currency _____
Markets   ☐ Global   ☐ _____   ☐ _____
               ☐ _____   ☐ _____   ☐ _____
Categories   1. _____
               2. _____
Keywords   1. _____
               2. _____
               3. _____
               4. _____
               5. _____
               6. _____
               7. _____
Book   _____
Description   _____
               _____
Book Cover   _____
Date First Sale ____/____/____   =   Q1   Q2   Q3   Q4
               ☐ Unpublished on ____/____/____

Title Details **71**

Title _____

Subtitle _____

ISBN _____ - _____

Book Type ☐ eBook ☐ Paperback
☐ Hardcover ☐ Audiobook
☐ Shareable PDF

Version _____ Edition _____

Series _____

Page Count _____ Trim Size _____ x _____

Date Published ___/___/___ = Q1 Q2 Q3 Q4

Publisher ☐ KDP ☐ KDP Print ☐ IngramSpark

Account(s) ☐ _____ ☐ _____
☐ _____ ☐ _____

Price $_____ Currency _____

Markets ☐ Global ☐ _____ ☐ _____
☐ _____ ☐ _____ ☐ _____

Categories 1. _____
2. _____

Keywords 1. _____
2. _____
3. _____
4. _____
5. _____
6. _____
7. _____

Book
Description _____
_____
_____

Book Cover _____

Date First Sale ___/___/___ = Q1 Q2 Q3 Q4
☐ Unpublished on ___/___/___

72

Title Details

Title   _____

Subtitle   _____

ISBN   _____ - _____

Book Type   ☐ eBook   ☐ Paperback
               ☐ Hardcover   ☐ Audiobook
               ☐ Shareable PDF

Version   _____ Edition _____

Series   _____

Page Count   _____ Trim Size _____ x _____

Date Published _____/_____/_____ = Q1   Q2   Q3   Q4

Publisher   ☐ KDP ☐ KDP Print   ☐ IngramSpark

Account(s)   ☐ _____   ☐ _____
               ☐ _____   ☐ _____

Price $_____ Currency _____

Markets   ☐ Global   ☐ _____   ☐ _____
               ☐ _____   ☐ _____   ☐ _____

Categories   1. _____
               2. _____

Keywords   1. _____
               2. _____
               3. _____
               4. _____
               5. _____
               6. _____
               7. _____

Book   _____
Description   _____
               _____
               _____

Book Cover   _____

Date First Sale _____/_____/_____ = Q1   Q2   Q3   Q4
                              ☐ Unpublished on _____/_____/_____

Title Details

Title _____

Subtitle _____

ISBN _____ - _____

Book Type ☐ eBook ☐ Paperback
☐ Hardcover ☐ Audiobook
☐ Shareable PDF

Version _____ Edition _____

Series _____

Page Count _____ Trim Size _____ x _____

Date Published ____/____/____ = Q1 Q2 Q3 Q4

Publisher ☐ KDP ☐ KDP Print ☐ IngramSpark

Account(s) ☐ _____ ☐ _____
☐ _____ ☐ _____

Price $_____ Currency _____

Markets ☐ Global ☐ _____ ☐ _____
☐ _____ ☐ _____ ☐ _____

Categories 1. _____
2. _____

Keywords 1. _____
2. _____
3. _____
4. _____
5. _____
6. _____
7. _____

Book _____

Description _____

_____

Book Cover _____

Date First Sale ____/____/____ = Q1 Q2 Q3 Q4
☐ Unpublished on ____/____/____

74

Title Details

Title _____

Subtitle _____

ISBN _____ - _____

Book Type   ☐ eBook   ☐ Paperback

                 ☐ Hardcover   ☐ Audiobook

                 ☐ Shareable PDF

Version _____ Edition _____

Series _____

Page Count _____ Trim Size _____ x _____

Date Published ____/____/____ =   Q1   Q2   Q3   Q4

Publisher   ☐ KDP   ☐ KDP Print   ☐ IngramSpark

Account(s)   ☐ _____   ☐ _____

             ☐ _____   ☐ _____

Price $_____ Currency _____

Markets   ☐ Global   ☐ _____   ☐ _____

         ☐ _____   ☐ _____   ☐ _____

Categories   1. _____

            2. _____

Keywords   1. _____

          2. _____

          3. _____

          4. _____

          5. _____

          6. _____

          7. _____

Book _____

Description _____

_____

Book Cover _____

Date First Sale ____/____/____ =   Q1   Q2   Q3   Q4

                        ☐ Unpublished on ____/____/____

Title Details

Title _____

Subtitle _____

ISBN _____ - _____

Book Type
☐ eBook ☐ Paperback
☐ Hardcover ☐ Audiobook
☐ Shareable PDF

Version _____ Edition _____

Series _____

Page Count _____ Trim Size _____ x _____

Date Published ____/____/____ = Q1 Q2 Q3 Q4

Publisher ☐ KDP ☐ KDP Print ☐ IngramSpark

Account(s)
☐ _____ ☐ _____
☐ _____ ☐ _____

Price $_____ Currency _____

Markets
☐ Global ☐ _____ ☐ _____
☐ _____ ☐ _____ ☐ _____

Categories
1. _____
2. _____

Keywords
1. _____
2. _____
3. _____
4. _____
5. _____
6. _____
7. _____

Book
Description
_____
_____
_____

Book Cover _____

Date First Sale ____/____/____ = Q1 Q2 Q3 Q4
☐ Unpublished on ____/____/____

76   **Title Details**

Title   _____

Subtitle   _____

ISBN   _____ - _____

Book Type   ☐ eBook   ☐ Paperback
             ☐ Hardcover   ☐ Audiobook
             ☐ Shareable PDF

Version _____ Edition _____

Series _____

Page Count _____ Trim Size _____ x _____

Date Published ___/___/___ = Q1   Q2   Q3   Q4

Publisher ☐ KDP ☐ KDP Print ☐ IngramSpark

Account(s) ☐ _____   ☐ _____
          ☐ _____   ☐ _____

Price $_____ Currency _____

Markets ☐ Global ☐ _____ ☐ _____
        ☐ _____ ☐ _____ ☐ _____

Categories
1. _____
2. _____

Keywords
1. _____
2. _____
3. _____
4. _____
5. _____
6. _____
7. _____

Book Description _____
_____
_____

Book Cover _____

Date First Sale ___/___/___ = Q1   Q2   Q3   Q4
☐ Unpublished on ___/___/___

Title Details

Title _____

Subtitle _____

ISBN _____ - _____

Book Type ☐ eBook   ☐ Paperback
☐ Hardcover   ☐ Audiobook
☐ Shareable PDF

Version _____ Edition _____

Series _____

Page Count _____ Trim Size _____ x _____

Date Published ____/____/____ = Q1   Q2   Q3   Q4

Publisher ☐ KDP   ☐ KDP Print   ☐ IngramSpark

Account(s) ☐ _____   ☐ _____
☐ _____   ☐ _____

Price $_____ Currency _____

Markets ☐ Global   ☐ _____   ☐ _____
☐ _____   ☐ _____   ☐ _____

Categories 1. _____
2. _____

Keywords 1. _____
2. _____
3. _____
4. _____
5. _____
6. _____
7. _____

Book
Description _____
_____
_____

Book Cover _____

Date First Sale ____/____/____ = Q1   Q2   Q3   Q4
☐ Unpublished on ____/____/____

78

Title Details

Title _____

Subtitle _____

ISBN _____ - _____

Book Type   ☐ eBook   ☐ Paperback

                ☐ Hardcover   ☐ Audiobook

                ☐ Shareable PDF

Version _____ Edition _____

Series _____

Page Count _____ Trim Size _____ x _____

Date Published ____/____/____ =   Q1   Q2   Q3   Q4

Publisher   ☐ KDP   ☐ KDP Print   ☐ IngramSpark

Account(s)   ☐ _____   ☐ _____

              ☐ _____   ☐ _____

Price $_____ Currency _____

Markets   ☐ Global   ☐ _____   ☐ _____

        ☐ _____   ☐ _____   ☐ _____

Categories   1. _____

           2. _____

Keywords   1. _____

           2. _____

           3. _____

           4. _____

           5. _____

           6. _____

           7. _____

Book _____

Description _____

_____

Book Cover _____

Date First Sale ____/____/____ =   Q1   Q2   Q3   Q4

                  ☐ Unpublished on ____/____/____

Title Details

Title _____

Subtitle _____

ISBN _____ - _____

Book Type ☐ eBook ☐ Paperback
☐ Hardcover ☐ Audiobook
☐ Shareable PDF

Version _____ Edition _____

Series _____

Page Count _____ Trim Size _____ x _____

Date Published ____/____/____ = Q1 Q2 Q3 Q4

Publisher ☐ KDP ☐ KDP Print ☐ IngramSpark

Account(s) ☐ _____ ☐ _____
☐ _____ ☐ _____

Price $_____ Currency _____

Markets ☐ Global ☐ _____ ☐ _____
☐ _____ ☐ _____ ☐ _____

Categories 1. _____
2. _____

Keywords 1. _____
2. _____
3. _____
4. _____
5. _____
6. _____
7. _____

Book Description _____
_____
_____

Book Cover _____

Date First Sale ____/____/____ = Q1 Q2 Q3 Q4
☐ Unpublished on ____/____/____

80 **Title Details**

Title _____

Subtitle _____

ISBN _____ - _____

Book Type
☐ eBook ☐ Paperback
☐ Hardcover ☐ Audiobook
☐ Shareable PDF

Version _____ Edition _____

Series _____

Page Count _____ Trim Size _____ x _____

Date Published ____/____/____ = Q1 Q2 Q3 Q4

Publisher ☐ KDP ☐ KDP Print ☐ IngramSpark

Account(s)
☐ _____ ☐ _____
☐ _____ ☐ _____

Price $_____ Currency _____

Markets
☐ Global ☐ _____ ☐ _____
☐ _____ ☐ _____ ☐ _____

Categories
1. _____
2. _____

Keywords
1. _____
2. _____
3. _____
4. _____
5. _____
6. _____
7. _____

Book
Description
_____
_____
_____

Book Cover _____

Date First Sale ____/____/____ = Q1 Q2 Q3 Q4
☐ Unpublished on ____/____/____

Title Details

Title _____

Subtitle _____

ISBN _____ - _____

Book Type   □ eBook   □ Paperback

               □ Hardcover   □ Audiobook

               □ Shareable PDF

Version _____ Edition _____

Series _____

Page Count _____ Trim Size _____ x _____

Date Published ____/____/____ = Q1   Q2   Q3   Q4

Publisher   □ KDP   □ KDP Print   □ IngramSpark

Account(s)   □ _____   □ _____

              □ _____   □ _____

Price   \$_____ Currency _____

Markets   □ Global   □ _____   □ _____

         □ _____   □ _____   □ _____

Categories

1. _____
2. _____

Keywords

1. _____
2. _____
3. _____
4. _____
5. _____
6. _____
7. _____

Book
Description

_____
_____
_____

Book Cover _____

Date First Sale ____/____/____ = Q1   Q2   Q3   Q4

                    □ Unpublished on ____/____/____

82   **Title Details**

Title _____

Subtitle _____

ISBN _____ - _____

Book Type   ☐ eBook   ☐ Paperback
           ☐ Hardcover   ☐ Audiobook
           ☐ Shareable PDF

Version _____ Edition _____

Series _____

Page Count _____ Trim Size _____ x _____

Date Published ___/___/___ =   Q1   Q2   Q3   Q4

Publisher   ☐ KDP   ☐ KDP Print   ☐ IngramSpark

Account(s)   ☐ _____   ☐ _____
          ☐ _____   ☐ _____

Price $_____ Currency _____

Markets   ☐ Global   ☐ _____   ☐ _____
        ☐ _____   ☐ _____   ☐ _____

Categories
1. _____
2. _____

Keywords
1. _____
2. _____
3. _____
4. _____
5. _____
6. _____
7. _____

Book
Description _____
_____
_____

Book Cover _____

Date First Sale ___/___/___ =   Q1   Q2   Q3   Q4
              ☐ Unpublished on ___/___/___

Title Details

Title _____

Subtitle _____

ISBN _____ - _____

Book Type   □ eBook   □ Paperback
            □ Hardcover   □ Audiobook
            □ Shareable PDF

Version _____   Edition _____

Series _____

Page Count _____   Trim Size _____ x _____

Date Published _____/_____/_____   =   Q1   Q2   Q3   Q4

Publisher   □ KDP   □ KDP Print   □ IngramSpark

Account(s)   □ _____   □ _____
             □ _____   □ _____

Price $_____   Currency _____

Markets   □ Global   □ _____   □ _____
          □ _____   □ _____   □ _____

Categories   1. _____
             2. _____

Keywords   1. _____
             2. _____
             3. _____
             4. _____
             5. _____
             6. _____
             7. _____

Book
Description _____
            _____
            _____

Book Cover _____

Date First Sale _____/_____/_____   =   Q1   Q2   Q3   Q4
                □ Unpublished on _____/_____/_____

84

Title Details

Title _____

Subtitle _____

ISBN _____ - _____

Book Type   ☐ eBook   ☐ Paperback

               ☐ Hardcover   ☐ Audiobook

               ☐ Shareable PDF

Version _____ Edition _____

Series _____

Page Count _____ Trim Size _____ x _____

Date Published ____/____/____ =   Q1   Q2   Q3   Q4

Publisher   ☐ KDP   ☐ KDP Print   ☐ IngramSpark

Account(s)   ☐ _____   ☐ _____

            ☐ _____   ☐ _____

Price $_____ Currency _____

Markets   ☐ Global   ☐ _____   ☐ _____

         ☐ _____   ☐ _____   ☐ _____

Categories   1. _____

          2. _____

Keywords   1. _____

          2. _____

          3. _____

          4. _____

          5. _____

          6. _____

          7. _____

Book _____

Description _____

_____

Book Cover _____

Date First Sale ____/____/____ =   Q1   Q2   Q3   Q4

                       ☐ Unpublished on ____/____/____

Title Details **85**

Title _____

Subtitle _____

ISBN _____ - _____

Book Type
- ☐ eBook ☐ Paperback
- ☐ Hardcover ☐ Audiobook
- ☐ Shareable PDF

Version _____ Edition _____

Series _____

Page Count _____ Trim Size _____ x _____

Date Published ____/____/____ = Q1   Q2   Q3   Q4

Publisher ☐ KDP ☐ KDP Print ☐ IngramSpark

Account(s)
- ☐ _____ ☐ _____
- ☐ _____ ☐ _____

Price \$_____ Currency _____

Markets
- ☐ Global ☐ _____ ☐ _____
- ☐ _____ ☐ _____ ☐ _____

Categories
1. _____
2. _____

Keywords
1. _____
2. _____
3. _____
4. _____
5. _____
6. _____
7. _____

Book
Description _____

 _____

 _____

Book Cover _____

Date First Sale ____/____/____ = Q1   Q2   Q3   Q4

☐ Unpublished on ____/____/____

86

Title Details

Title   _____

Subtitle   _____

ISBN   _____ - _____

Book Type   ☐ eBook   ☐ Paperback

               ☐ Hardcover   ☐ Audiobook

               ☐ Shareable PDF

Version   _____   Edition   _____

Series   _____

Page Count   _____   Trim Size   _____ x _____

Date Published   ____/____/____   =   Q1   Q2   Q3   Q4

Publisher   ☐ KDP   ☐ KDP Print   ☐ IngramSpark

Account(s)   ☐ _____   ☐ _____

              ☐ _____   ☐ _____

Price $_____   Currency _____

Markets   ☐ Global   ☐ _____   ☐ _____

           ☐ _____   ☐ _____   ☐ _____

Categories   1. _____

            2. _____

Keywords   1. _____

            2. _____

            3. _____

            4. _____

            5. _____

            6. _____

            7. _____

Book   _____

Description   _____

            _____

Book Cover   _____

Date First Sale   ____/____/____   =   Q1   Q2   Q3   Q4

                            ☐ Unpublished on ____/____/____

Title Details

Title _____

Subtitle _____

ISBN _____ - _____

Book Type
☐ eBook ☐ Paperback
☐ Hardcover ☐ Audiobook
☐ Shareable PDF

Version _____ Edition _____

Series _____

Page Count _____ Trim Size _____ x _____

Date Published ____/____/____ = Q1 Q2 Q3 Q4

Publisher ☐ KDP ☐ KDP Print ☐ IngramSpark

Account(s)
☐ _____ ☐ _____
☐ _____ ☐ _____

Price $_____ Currency _____

Markets
☐ Global ☐ _____ ☐ _____
☐ _____ ☐ _____ ☐ _____

Categories
1. _____
2. _____

Keywords
1. _____
2. _____
3. _____
4. _____
5. _____
6. _____
7. _____

Book
Description
_____
_____
_____

Book Cover _____

Date First Sale ____/____/____ = Q1 Q2 Q3 Q4
☐ Unpublished on ____/____/____

88 **Title Details**

Title _____

Subtitle _____

ISBN _____ - _____

Book Type ☐ eBook ☐ Paperback

☐ Hardcover ☐ Audiobook

☐ Shareable PDF

Version _____ Edition _____

Series _____

Page Count _____ Trim Size _____ x _____

Date Published ____/____/____ = Q1   Q2   Q3   Q4

Publisher ☐ KDP ☐ KDP Print ☐ IngramSpark

Account(s) ☐ _____ ☐ _____

☐ _____ ☐ _____

Price $_____ Currency _____

Markets ☐ Global ☐ _____ ☐ _____

☐ _____ ☐ _____ ☐ _____

Categories 1. _____

2. _____

Keywords 1. _____

2. _____

3. _____

4. _____

5. _____

6. _____

7. _____

Book _____

Description _____

_____

Book Cover _____

Date First Sale ____/____/____ = Q1   Q2   Q3   Q4

☐ Unpublished on ____/____/____

Title Details   **89**

Title   _____

Subtitle   _____

ISBN   _____ - _____

Book Type   ☐ eBook   ☐ Paperback
                 ☐ Hardcover   ☐ Audiobook
                 ☐ Shareable PDF

Version   _____   Edition _____

Series   _____

Page Count   _____   Trim Size   _____ x _____

Date Published   ____/____/____ = Q1   Q2   Q3   Q4

Publisher   ☐ KDP   ☐ KDP Print   ☐ IngramSpark

Account(s)   ☐ _____   ☐ _____
                 ☐ _____   ☐ _____

Price $_____ Currency _____

Markets   ☐ Global   ☐ _____   ☐ _____
                 ☐ _____ ☐ _____   ☐ _____

Categories   1. _____
                 2. _____

Keywords   1. _____
                 2. _____
                 3. _____
                 4. _____
                 5. _____
                 6. _____
                 7. _____

Book   _____
Description   _____
                 _____

Book Cover   _____

Date First Sale ____/____/____ = Q1   Q2   Q3   Q4
                 ☐ Unpublished on ____/____/____

90   **Title Details**

Title   _____

Subtitle   _____

ISBN   _____ - _____

Book Type   ☐ eBook   ☐ Paperback
     ☐ Hardcover   ☐ Audiobook
     ☐ Shareable PDF

Version _____ Edition _____

Series _____

Page Count _____ Trim Size _____ x _____

Date Published ____/____/____ =   Q1   Q2   Q3   Q4

Publisher ☐ KDP   ☐ KDP Print   ☐ IngramSpark

Account(s) ☐ _____   ☐ _____
     ☐ _____   ☐ _____

Price $_____ Currency _____

Markets ☐ Global   ☐ _____   ☐ _____
     ☐ _____   ☐ _____   ☐ _____

Categories
1. _____
2. _____

Keywords
1. _____
2. _____
3. _____
4. _____
5. _____
6. _____
7. _____

Book
Description
_____
_____
_____

Book Cover _____

Date First Sale ____/____/____ =   Q1   Q2   Q3   Q4
     ☐ Unpublished on ____/____/____

Title Details

Title _____

Subtitle _____

ISBN _____ - _____

Book Type ☐ eBook ☐ Paperback
☐ Hardcover ☐ Audiobook
☐ Shareable PDF

Version _____ Edition _____

Series _____

Page Count _____ Trim Size _____ x _____

Date Published ____/____/____ = Q1 Q2 Q3 Q4

Publisher ☐ KDP ☐ KDP Print ☐ IngramSpark

Account(s) ☐ _____ ☐ _____
☐ _____ ☐ _____

Price $_____ Currency _____

Markets ☐ Global ☐ _____ ☐ _____
☐ _____ ☐ _____ ☐ _____

Categories 1. _____
2. _____

Keywords 1. _____
2. _____
3. _____
4. _____
5. _____
6. _____
7. _____

Book _____

Description _____
_____

Book Cover _____

Date First Sale ____/____/____ = Q1 Q2 Q3 Q4
☐ Unpublished on ____/____/____

92

Title Details

Title _____

Subtitle _____

ISBN _____ - _____

Book Type ☐ eBook   ☐ Paperback
          ☐ Hardcover   ☐ Audiobook
          ☐ Shareable PDF

Version _____ Edition _____

Series _____

Page Count _____ Trim Size _____ x _____

Date Published ____/____/____ = Q1 Q2 Q3 Q4

Publisher ☐ KDP ☐ KDP Print ☐ IngramSpark

Account(s) ☐ _____   ☐ _____
           ☐ _____   ☐ _____

Price $_____ Currency _____

Markets ☐ Global   ☐ _____ ☐ _____
        ☐ _____ ☐ _____ ☐ _____

Categories 1. _____
           2. _____

Keywords 1. _____
         2. _____
         3. _____
         4. _____
         5. _____
         6. _____
         7. _____

Book _____

Description _____

_____

Book Cover _____

Date First Sale ____/____/____ = Q1 Q2 Q3 Q4

☐ Unpublished on ____/____/____

Title Details   **93**

Title _____

Subtitle _____

ISBN _____ - _____

Book Type
☐ eBook   ☐ Paperback
☐ Hardcover   ☐ Audiobook
☐ Shareable PDF

Version _____ Edition _____

Series _____

Page Count _____ Trim Size _____ x _____

Date Published ____/____/____ = | Q1 | Q2 | Q3 | Q4 |

Publisher ☐ KDP ☐ KDP Print ☐ IngramSpark

Account(s)
☐ _____   ☐ _____
☐ _____   ☐ _____

Price $_____ Currency _____

Markets
☐ Global   ☐ _____   ☐ _____
☐ _____   ☐ _____   ☐ _____

Categories
1. _____
2. _____

Keywords
1. _____
2. _____
3. _____
4. _____
5. _____
6. _____
7. _____

Book
Description
_____
_____
_____

Book Cover _____

Date First Sale ____/____/____ = | Q1 | Q2 | Q3 | Q4 |

☐ Unpublished on ____/____/____

94   **Title Details**

Title   _____

Subtitle   _____

ISBN   _____ - _____

Book Type   ☐ eBook   ☐ Paperback

               ☐ Hardcover   ☐ Audiobook

               ☐ Shareable PDF

Version   _____ Edition   _____

Series   _____

Page Count   _____ Trim Size   _____ x _____

Date Published   _____/_____/_____ = Q1   Q2   Q3   Q4

Publisher   ☐ KDP   ☐ KDP Print   ☐ IngramSpark

Account(s)   ☐ _____   ☐ _____

              ☐ _____   ☐ _____

Price $_____ Currency _____

Markets   ☐ Global   ☐ _____   ☐ _____

         ☐ _____   ☐ _____   ☐ _____

Categories   1. _____

         2. _____

Keywords   1. _____

         2. _____

         3. _____

         4. _____

         5. _____

         6. _____

         7. _____

Book   _____

Description   _____

         _____

Book Cover   _____

Date First Sale   _____/_____/_____ = Q1   Q2   Q3   Q4

                         ☐ Unpublished on _____/_____/_____

Title Details

Title   _____

Subtitle   _____

ISBN   _____ - _____

Book Type

☐ eBook   ☐ Paperback

☐ Hardcover   ☐ Audiobook

☐ Shareable PDF

Version   _____   Edition   _____

Series   _____

Page Count   _____   Trim Size   _____ x _____

Date Published   ____/____/____   =   Q1   Q2   Q3   Q4

Publisher   ☐ KDP   ☐ KDP Print   ☐ IngramSpark

Account(s)   ☐ _____   ☐ _____

            ☐ _____   ☐ _____

Price $_____   Currency _____

Markets   ☐ Global   ☐ _____   ☐ _____

         ☐ _____   ☐ _____   ☐ _____

Categories

1. _____

2. _____

Keywords

1. _____

2. _____

3. _____

4. _____

5. _____

6. _____

7. _____

Book Description   _____

           _____

           _____

Book Cover   _____

Date First Sale   ____/____/____   =   Q1   Q2   Q3   Q4

           ☐ Unpublished on ____/____/____

96   **Title Details**

Title   _____

Subtitle   _____

ISBN   _____ - _____

Book Type   ☐ eBook   ☐ Paperback

      ☐ Hardcover   ☐ Audiobook

      ☐ Shareable PDF

Version   _____ Edition _____

Series   _____

Page Count   _____ Trim Size _____ x _____

Date Published   ____/____/____   =   Q1   Q2   Q3   Q4

Publisher   ☐ KDP   ☐ KDP Print   ☐ IngramSpark

Account(s)   ☐ _____   ☐ _____

      ☐ _____   ☐ _____

Price $_____ Currency _____

Markets   ☐ Global   ☐ _____   ☐ _____

      ☐ _____   ☐ _____   ☐ _____

Categories   1. _____

      2. _____

Keywords   1. _____

      2. _____

      3. _____

      4. _____

      5. _____

      6. _____

      7. _____

Book   _____

Description   _____

      _____

Book Cover   _____

Date First Sale   ____/____/____   =   Q1   Q2   Q3   Q4

      ☐ Unpublished on ____/____/____

Title Details

Title _____

Subtitle _____

ISBN _____ - _____

Book Type ☐ eBook ☐ Paperback
☐ Hardcover ☐ Audiobook
☐ Shareable PDF

Version _____ Edition _____

Series _____

Page Count _____ Trim Size _____ x _____

Date Published _____/_____/_____ = Q1 Q2 Q3 Q4

Publisher ☐ KDP ☐ KDP Print ☐ IngramSpark

Account(s) ☐ _____ ☐ _____
☐ _____ ☐ _____

Price $_____ Currency _____

Markets ☐ Global ☐ _____ ☐ _____
☐ _____ ☐ _____ ☐ _____

Categories 1. _____
2. _____

Keywords 1. _____
2. _____
3. _____
4. _____
5. _____
6. _____
7. _____

Book _____

Description _____
_____

Book Cover _____

Date First Sale _____/_____/_____ = Q1 Q2 Q3 Q4
☐ Unpublished on _____/_____/_____

98

Title Details

Title _____

Subtitle _____

ISBN _____ - _____

Book Type   ☐ eBook   ☐ Paperback
             ☐ Hardcover   ☐ Audiobook
             ☐ Shareable PDF

Version _____ Edition _____

Series _____

Page Count _____ Trim Size _____ x _____

Date Published ____/____/____ = Q1   Q2   Q3   Q4

Publisher   ☐ KDP   ☐ KDP Print   ☐ IngramSpark

Account(s)   ☐ _____   ☐ _____
            ☐ _____   ☐ _____

Price $_____ Currency _____

Markets   ☐ Global   ☐ _____   ☐ _____
         ☐ _____   ☐ _____   ☐ _____

Categories   1. _____
           2. _____

Keywords   1. _____
          2. _____
          3. _____
          4. _____
          5. _____
          6. _____
          7. _____

Book _____

Description _____

_____

Book Cover _____

Date First Sale ____/____/____ = Q1   Q2   Q3   Q4

                     ☐ Unpublished on ____/____/____

Title Details

Title _____

Subtitle _____

ISBN _____ - _____

Book Type ☐ eBook ☐ Paperback
☐ Hardcover ☐ Audiobook
☐ Shareable PDF

Version _____ Edition _____

Series _____

Page Count _____ Trim Size _____ x _____

Date Published ____/____/____ = Q1 Q2 Q3 Q4

Publisher ☐ KDP ☐ KDP Print ☐ IngramSpark

Account(s) ☐ _____ ☐ _____
☐ _____ ☐ _____

Price $_____ Currency _____

Markets ☐ Global ☐ _____ ☐ _____
☐ _____ ☐ _____ ☐ _____

Categories 1. _____
2. _____

Keywords 1. _____
2. _____
3. _____
4. _____
5. _____
6. _____
7. _____

Book _____
Description _____
_____

Book Cover _____

Date First Sale ____/____/____ = Q1 Q2 Q3 Q4
☐ Unpublished on ____/____/____

100   **Title Details**

Title   _____

Subtitle   _____

ISBN   _____ - _____

Book Type   ☐ eBook   ☐ Paperback

     ☐ Hardcover   ☐ Audiobook

     ☐ Shareable PDF

Version   _____ Edition _____

Series   _____

Page Count   _____ Trim Size _____ x _____

Date Published   _____/_____/_____ = Q1   Q2   Q3   Q4

Publisher   ☐ KDP   ☐ KDP Print   ☐ IngramSpark

Account(s)   ☐ _____   ☐ _____

     ☐ _____   ☐ _____

Price $_____ Currency _____

Markets   ☐ Global   ☐ _____   ☐ _____

     ☐ _____   ☐ _____   ☐ _____

Categories   1. _____

     2. _____

Keywords   1. _____

     2. _____

     3. _____

     4. _____

     5. _____

     6. _____

     7. _____

Book   _____

Description   _____

     _____

     _____

Book Cover   _____

Date First Sale   _____/_____/_____ = Q1   Q2   Q3   Q4

     ☐ Unpublished on _____/_____/_____

Sales
tracking

Book Sales

Year: _____ Channel	Q1			Q2		
	Jan	Feb	Mar	Apr	May	Jun
KDP (Kindle)	#	#	#	#	#	#
	$	$	$	$	$	$
KDP (Print)	#	#	#	#	#	#
	$	$	$	$	$	$
IngramSpark	#	#	#	#	#	#
	$	$	$	$	$	$
	#	#	#	#	#	#
	$	$	$	$	$	$
	#	#	#	#	#	#
	$	$	$	$	$	$
	#	#	#	#	#	#
	$	$	$	$	$	$
	#	#	#	#	#	#
	$	$	$	$	$	$
	#	#	#	#	#	#
	$	$	$	$	$	$
	#	#	#	#	#	#
	$	$	$	$	$	$
	#	#	#	#	#	#
	$	$	$	$	$	$
	#	#	#	#	#	#
	$	$	$	$	$	$
	#	#	#	#	#	#
	$	$	$	$	$	$
	#	#	#	#	#	#
	$	$	$	$	$	$
	#	#	#	#	#	#
	$	$	$	$	$	$
	#	#	#	#	#	#
	$	$	$	$	$	$
Monthly TOTALS	#	#	#	#	#	#
	$	$	$	$	$	$

Book Sales

Q3			Q4			Yearly Totals
Jul	Aug	Sept	Oct	Nov	Dec	
#	#	#	#	#	#`	
$	$	$	$	$	$	
#	#	#	#	#	#	
$	$	$	$	$	$	
#	#	#	#	#	#	
$	$	$	$	$	$	
#	#	#	#	#	#	
$	$	$	$	$	$	
#	#	#	#	#	#	
$	$	$	$	$	$	
#	#	#	#	#	#	
$	$	$	$	$	$	
#	#	#	#	#	#	
$	$	$	$	$	$	
#	#	#	#	#	#	
$	$	$	$	$	$	
#	#	#	#	#	#	
$	$	$	$	$	$	
#	#	#	#	#	#	
$	$	$	$	$	$	
#	#	#	#	#	#	
$	$	$	$	$	$	
#	#	#	#	#	#	
$	$	$	$	$	$	
#	#	#	#	#	#	
$	$	$	$	$	$	
#	#	#	#	#	#	
$	$	$	$	$	$	

Book Sales

Year: _____ Channel	Q1			Q2		
	Jan	Feb	Mar	Apr	May	Jun
KDP (Kindle)	#	#	#	#	#	#
	$	$	$	$	$	$
KDP (Print)	#	#	#	#	#	#
	$	$	$	$	$	$
IngramSpark	#	#	#	#	#	#
	$	$	$	$	$	$
	#	#	#	#	#	#
	$	$	$	$	$	$
	#	#	#	#	#	#
	$	$	$	$	$	$
	#	#	#	#	#	#
	$	$	$	$	$	$
	#	#	#	#	#	#
	$	$	$	$	$	$
	#	#	#	#	#	#
	$	$	$	$	$	$
	#	#	#	#	#	#
	$	$	$	$	$	$
	#	#	#	#	#	#
	$	$	$	$	$	$
	#	#	#	#	#	#
	$	$	$	$	$	$
	#	#	#	#	#	#
	$	$	$	$	$	$
	#	#	#	#	#	#
	$	$	$	$	$	$
	#	#	#	#	#	#
	$	$	$	$	$	$
Monthly TOTALS	#	#	#	#	#	#
	$	$	$	$	$	$

Book Sales

Q3			Q4			Yearly Totals
Jul	**Aug**	**Sept**	**Oct**	**Nov**	**Dec**	
#	#	#	#	#	#`	
$	$	$	$	$	$	
#	#	#	#	#	#	
$	$	$	$	$	$	
#	#	#	#	#	#	
$	$	$	$	$	$	
#	#	#	#	#	#	
$	$	$	$	$	$	
#	#	#	#	#	#	
$	$	$	$	$	$	
#	#	#	#	#	#	
$	$	$	$	$	$	
#	#	#	#	#	#	
$	$	$	$	$	$	
#	#	#	#	#	#	
$	$	$	$	$	$	
#	#	#	#	#	#	
$	$	$	$	$	$	
#	#	#	#	#	#	
$	$	$	$	$	$	
#	#	#	#	#	#	
$	$	$	$	$	$	
#	#	#	#	#	#	
$	$	$	$	$	$	
#	#	#	#	#	#	
$	$	$	$	$	$	
#	#	#	#	#	#	
$	$	$	$	$	$	

Self-Published Books Tracker

Book Sales

Year: _____

Channel	Q1			Q2		
	Jan	Feb	Mar	Apr	May	Jun
KDP (Kindle)	#	#	#	#	#	#
	$	$	$	$	$	$
KDP (Print)	#	#	#	#	#	#
	$	$	$	$	$	$
IngramSpark	#	#	#	#	#	#
	$	$	$	$	$	$
	#	#	#	#	#	#
	$	$	$	$	$	$
	#	#	#	#	#	#
	$	$	$	$	$	$
	#	#	#	#	#	#
	$	$	$	$	$	$
	#	#	#	#	#	#
	$	$	$	$	$	$
	#	#	#	#	#	#
	$	$	$	$	$	$
	#	#	#	#	#	#
	$	$	$	$	$	$
	#	#	#	#	#	#
	$	$	$	$	$	$
	#	#	#	#	#	#
	$	$	$	$	$	$
	#	#	#	#	#	#
	$	$	$	$	$	$
	#	#	#	#	#	#
	$	$	$	$	$	$
Monthly TOTALS	#	#	#	#	#	#
	$	$	$	$	$	$

Book Sales

Q3			Q4			Yearly Totals
Jul	Aug	Sept	Oct	Nov	Dec	
#	#	#	#	#	#`	
$	$	$	$	$	$	
#	#	#	#	#	#	
$	$	$	$	$	$	
#	#	#	#	#	#	
$	$	$	$	$	$	
#	#	#	#	#	#	
$	$	$	$	$	$	
#	#	#	#	#	#	
$	$	$	$	$	$	
#	#	#	#	#	#	
$	$	$	$	$	$	
#	#	#	#	#	#	
$	$	$	$	$	$	
#	#	#	#	#	#	
$	$	$	$	$	$	
#	#	#	#	#	#	
$	$	$	$	$	$	
#	#	#	#	#	#	
$	$	$	$	$	$	
#	#	#	#	#	#	
$	$	$	$	$	$	
#	#	#	#	#	#	
$	$	$	$	$	$	
#	#	#	#	#	#	
$	$	$	$	$	$	
#	#	#	#	#	#	
$	$	$	$	$	$	

Book Sales

Channel	Q1			Q2		
Year: _____	Jan	Feb	Mar	Apr	May	Jun
KDP (Kindle)	#	#	#	#	#	#
	$	$	$	$	$	$
KDP (Print)	#	#	#	#	#	#
	$	$	$	$	$	$
IngramSpark	#	#	#	#	#	#
	$	$	$	$	$	$
	#	#	#	#	#	#
	$	$	$	$	$	$
	#	#	#	#	#	#
	$	$	$	$	$	$
	#	#	#	#	#	#
	$	$	$	$	$	$
	#	#	#	#	#	#
	$	$	$	$	$	$
	#	#	#	#	#	#
	$	$	$	$	$	$
	#	#	#	#	#	#
	$	$	$	$	$	$
	#	#	#	#	#	#
	$	$	$	$	$	$
	#	#	#	#	#	#
	$	$	$	$	$	$
	#	#	#	#	#	#
	$	$	$	$	$	$
	#	#	#	#	#	#
	$	$	$	$	$	$
Monthly TOTALS	#	#	#	#	#	#
	$	$	$	$	$	$

Book Sales

Q3			Q4			Yearly Totals
Jul	**Aug**	**Sept**	**Oct**	**Nov**	**Dec**	
#	#	#	#	#	#`	
$	$	$	$	$	$	
#	#	#	#	#	#	
$	$	$	$	$	$	
#	#	#	#	#	#	
$	$	$	$	$	$	
#	#	#	#	#	#	
$	$	$	$	$	$	
#	#	#	#	#	#	
$	$	$	$	$	$	
#	#	#	#	#	#	
$	$	$	$	$	$	
#	#	#	#	#	#	
$	$	$	$	$	$	
#	#	#	#	#	#	
$	$	$	$	$	$	
#	#	#	#	#	#	
$	$	$	$	$	$	
#	#	#	#	#	#	
$	$	$	$	$	$	
#	#	#	#	#	#	
$	$	$	$	$	$	
#	#	#	#	#	#	
$	$	$	$	$	$	
#	#	#	#	#	#	
$	$	$	$	$	$	

Book Sales

Year: _____

Channel	Q1			Q2		
	Jan	Feb	Mar	Apr	May	Jun
KDP (Kindle)	#	#	#	#	#	#
	$	$	$	$	$	$
KDP (Print)	#	#	#	#	#	#
	$	$	$	$	$	$
IngramSpark	#	#	#	#	#	#
	$	$	$	$	$	$
	#	#	#	#	#	#
	$	$	$	$	$	$
	#	#	#	#	#	#
	$	$	$	$	$	$
	#	#	#	#	#	#
	$	$	$	$	$	$
	#	#	#	#	#	#
	$	$	$	$	$	$
	#	#	#	#	#	#
	$	$	$	$	$	$
	#	#	#	#	#	#
	$	$	$	$	$	$
	#	#	#	#	#	#
	$	$	$	$	$	$
	#	#	#	#	#	#
	$	$	$	$	$	$
	#	#	#	#	#	#
	$	$	$	$	$	$
	#	#	#	#	#	#
	$	$	$	$	$	$
	#	#	#	#	#	#
	$	$	$	$	$	$
	#	#	#	#	#	#
	$	$	$	$	$	$
Monthly TOTALS	#	#	#	#	#	#
	$	$	$	$	$	$

Book Sales

	Q3			Q4			
Jul	Aug	Sept	Oct	Nov	Dec		Yearly Totals
#	#	#	#	#	#`		
$	$	$	$	$	$		
#	#	#	#	#	#		
$	$	$	$	$	$		
#	#	#	#	#	#		
$	$	$	$	$	$		
#	#	#	#	#	#		
$	$	$	$	$	$		
#	#	#	#	#	#		
$	$	$	$	$	$		
#	#	#	#	#	#		
$	$	$	$	$	$		
#	#	#	#	#	#		
$	$	$	$	$	$		
#	#	#	#	#	#		
$	$	$	$	$	$		
#	#	#	#	#	#		
$	$	$	$	$	$		
#	#	#	#	#	#		
$	$	$	$	$	$		
#	#	#	#	#	#		
$	$	$	$	$	$		
#	#	#	#	#	#		
$	$	$	$	$	$		
#	#	#	#	#	#		
$	$	$	$	$	$		
#	#	#	#	#	#		
$	$	$	$	$	$		

eDiY Publishing

Visit our Amazon Page
amazon.com/author/ediypublishing

Visit our Facebook Page
facebook.com/eDiYPublishing

Other Books

Invisible Illness: Daily Symptoms Tracker

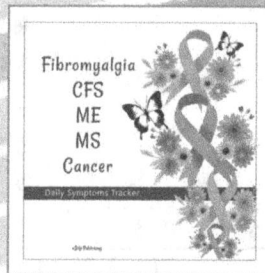

Fibromyalgia CFS ME MS Cancer: Daily Symptoms Tracker

Fuel Fillups Logbooks

www.ingramcontent.com/pod-product-compliance
Lightning Source LLC
Chambersburg PA
CBHW050229270326
41914CB00003BA/637